THE ART OF ENCOURAGEMENT

How you can encourage yourself
and other people

MIKE PEGG

ENHANCE LTD

Leamington Spa

First published in the United Kingdom in 1995 by
Enhance Ltd, The Hall, Radford Hall, Radford Semele,
Leamington Spa, CV31 1FH

British Library Cataloguing in Publication Data applied for.
ISBN 0-9521358-1-7

Design and origination by Magenta, Leamington Spa.
Printed and bound in Great Britain by Ebenezer Baylis, Worcester.

CONTENTS

Also by Mike Pegg:

Positive Leadership
The Positive Planet
The Positive Workbook

INTRODUCTION

EVERYBODY is an artist, everybody is creative, everybody can help to build a better world. Perhaps this view sounds naive, but it is tempered with realism. I believe in people, but only when they choose to do their best. During the past thirty years I have had the opportunity to work with people from many walks of life. They have taught me that, providing they are offered the basic materials for life:

People can choose to be positive

People can choose to be Encouragers, rather than Stoppers. They can be Creators, rather than Complainers. They can take responsibility for helping others, rather than simply walking past problems. They can take this path based on years of life-experience, wisdom and pain, rather than wide-eyed, naive simplicity. They can be on the side of Life, rather than Death.

People can choose to do positive work

People can choose to build on their strengths, rather than complain about their weaknesses. They can do good quality work that helps other people. They can strive to get the right balance between pursuing their mission and paying their mortgage. They can do their best, rather than fail to do their best. They can finish what they were born to finish.

People can choose to build a Positive Planet

People can choose to be Doers, rather than Talkers. They can do what they can do, rather than talk about what they can't do. They can be part of the solution, rather than part of the problem. They can make beautiful products, pass on their wisdom and give hope to future generations. They can combine their talents to build a Positive Planet.

Encouragers often take three steps towards helping people to do their best: they focus on Encouragement, Enterprise and Excellence. Sounds simple, but it isn't easy. This book describes the art of encouragement. It offers a philosophy and practical tools which readers can use to encourage themselves and others in their daily lives and work. It can be read as an ordinary book or used as a workbook by you and your colleagues. Please take the ideas you like best and use them to continue to be an Encourager.

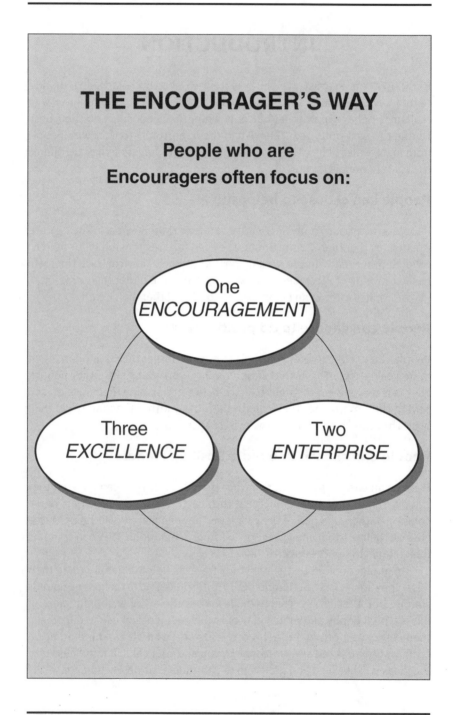

THE ENCOURAGER'S WAY

**People who are
Encouragers often focus on:**

One
ENCOURAGEMENT

Three
EXCELLENCE

Two
ENTERPRISE

Step One:
ENCOURAGEMENT

"WHAT has helped you to grow most in your life?" Time and again I asked people this question when I began running a community for troubled teenagers in 1968. Knowing little about therapy, I needed to learn quickly. The obvious way was to ask people what had helped them to develop: the next step would be recreate these conditions in the community. So I asked people from all walks of life: "What has helped you to grow?" They gave similar answers:

"I had somebody who encouraged me . . . My mother told me to believe in myself . . . My grandfather made me feel special . . . I had an English teacher who took an interest in me . . . My sports coach taught me always to do my best . . . I read a book which gave me hope . . . My partner gives me the space to develop my own life . . . I have been given lots of love during my life."

Encouragement cropped up time after time: so how could the community's staff be good Encouragers? We helped the teenagers to clarify their strengths, but we also asked them to take responsibility for achieving their aims in life. Why? Love is a good starting point, but it is not enough. People must also "get out of the chair" and translate their ideas into action. The teenagers who grew were those who worked to shape their futures. Encouragers do their best and invite others to do *their* best too.

Sheila Cassidy is an Encourager. The former Medical Director of St. Luke's Hospice in Plymouth, she believes professionals like herself must learn to show their love, rather than suppress their love. Hospices show that all people have value, not just the rich and beautiful. Writing in *Sharing the Darkness*, Sheila describes her first meeting with a patient:

"Once alone with a new patient I introduce myself, explain that I have come at the request of their doctor, and ask them to tell me their story . . . It is in the telling of the story that I meet my patient and in my listening to him that he meets me . . . Everything depends on the quality of my listening: the patient must understand clearly from my verbal and non-verbal cues that I am interested in him as a person as well as in his physical problems . . . I ask not only what happened and what the doctors said to him, but how he felt about it then — and how he feels now."

Sheila helps people to feel wanted and, if they wish, to face their future honestly. Caring calls for more than treating the illness. It calls for answering people's questions, sitting by their bedside, drawing diagrams and talking to angry relatives. Finally even the Medical Director must admit that she does not have the all-embracing power to cure. She is not God, but she can help people to face the darkness.

Encouragement is another name for love, and Sheila expresses this in her daily work. She talks of Frank, a Manchester builder, who suddenly became paralysed from the waist down. The cancer in his kidney reached his spine, and St. Luke's staff helped him to wrestle with his sense of loss: he would never walk again. Driving around Plymouth, Sheila reflects on her own personality, her strengths and limits. We all have talents; we all have weaknesses; we all have something to give to the world. She writes:

"I found myself saying again and again, 'You wash the feet that will not walk tomorrow', and realised that this was my job, my calling. I, who have little patience with the demented and no love for tiny babies, have a special gift of warmth and understanding for those whose time is running out. I, who hate parties and find it nigh impossible to make small talk, know instinctively what to say and do for a gentle Manchester builder who is facing the humiliation of incontinence and the fear of death."

Hospices have much to teach our society, says Sheila. They value the vulnerable: the brain-damaged, the sick and the old. They do this in a world that values competition and economic success. Vulnerability is a great teacher because it crystallises what is really important in our lives. Sheila is not talking about building more hospices. She is talking about expanding the hospice philosophy across society. All people are precious; all people need love; all people want to find peace in their lives.

"But isn't working with the dying depressing?" Joan Bakewell once asked her in a television programme. The camera stayed on Sheila, who thought for ten seconds. "Oh no," she finally replied, "but it is costly." How does she cope with the price to be paid? Sheila surrounds herself with beautiful colours, paintings and music.

YOU CAN ENCOURAGE YOURSELF

Caring people sometimes fail to take their own medicine. One of my former work colleagues was so duty-driven that he failed to take care of himself. One day I persuaded him to stay at home for two weeks, saying: "For goodness sake take a holiday — and we don't mean write another book. You're no use to us when you're exhausted." Two car crashes in a year finally taught him to hear the message.

Rollo May, the author of *The Courage to Create*, urged people to encourage themselves. Everybody has strengths, but some use their creativity more than others. Why? Courage calls for both self-encouragement and discipline.

Writing in **The Ageless Spirit,** Rollo explains that creativity keeps us moving forward. "You are never fully satisfied," he says. "You are always working and reworking your art, your book, your garden, whatever."

How can you find your talents? How can you keep the flame alive as you grow older? Rollo asks:

"What is it that you make? What is it that you do? When we think in those terms, then all of us are creative — we all do things, make things . . . I really think creativity is the answer to ageing, and by creativity I mean listening to one's own inner voice, to one's own ideas, to one's own aspirations. It may be social work. It may be gardening. It may be building. But it must be something fresh, some thing or an idea that takes fire — this is what I would like to see among older people."

Age brings wisdom, says Rollo. Older people can add their life-experience to the treasure chest of human knowledge. Creativity ebbs and flows, however, and they must learn to sail with the tide. Some artists have only two hours a day when they can create usefully, while the remaining hours are devoted to other work. Guard your prime time carefully and plan your days around these magical times, says Rollo, who adds:

"I stay in my studio each day for four hours, but the last hour and a half isn't worth very much. It was hard for me to accept, but what can I do? All I can do is make the most of the creative time I've got. So for two-and-a-half hours I'm moving marvellously; the rest of the time I'm simply fiddling around. But I find joy in fiddling too. I have to accept the fact that I'm not a God. I have to accept my destiny. I have to accept the fact that I can only do creative work for a few hours a day, but that does not diminish one iota the joy I get from those two hours."

How can you tap your own creative energy? You may wish to tackle the exercise on the next page and describe specific things you can do to encourage yourself. For example:

- Spend time with people who encourage me.
- Listen to music.
- Paint pictures.
- Walk in the forest.
- Organise my time so I can work on my life-goals.

Doing these things will recharge your batteries and stimulate you to take the next step towards supporting other people.

HOW I CAN
ENCOURAGE MYSELF

Write down the things you can do to recharge your batteries. For example: spending time with certain people, listening to music, walking in the country, making beautiful products or writing your thoughts in a journal. Doing these things will give you more energy to encourage other people.

● I can _____

_____

● I can _____

_____

● I can _____

_____

YOU CAN ENCOURAGE
OTHER PEOPLE

"You have to look for what Antoine St. Exupery called 'The Murdered Mozart' in each person," said George Lyward, a pioneer in child care. "Look for the golden moments when they 'come alive'. A person may be painting, playing football or whatever. Help them to discover what they are doing right. They will then be able to create more of those golden moments. Help the person to become the best kind of Mozart they can be."

George Lyward achieved outstanding results at Finchden Manor, a community for disturbed boys. Bus loads of social workers travelled into the Kent countryside to visit Finchden and seek the secret of his success. Walking around the community, they saw boys playing guitars, kicking footballs, building sheds, planting flowers and tackling school lessons. Finally the visitors crammed into the hall and bombarded George with questions. "What therapy do you believe in?" they asked, "What is the staff's role? They seem to do little except watch the boys."

"Our staff are talent spotters," George replied. "Watching is one of the hardest things to do in life. Our staff watch the boys painting, mending cars, gardening, studying science or whatever. Looking for when somebody 'comes alive', they nurture the boys' talent and educate them to find work they enjoy. Our task is to help the boys to find their true work in life."

George Lyward pursued his road towards helping people. How can you find your road? One way to begin is by recalling people who have inspired you during your life. If you wish, try the exercise called My Encouragers. Start by writing the names of the people who have encouraged you. My list would include, for example:

- My mother and father.
- Mrs Peel, my English teacher at school.
- Abraham Maslow, whom I never met, but whose books gave me a new view of human possibilities.
- Alec Dickson, one of my mentors.

Now tackle the second part of the exercise. What did each person do right to give you encouragement? For example: Having failed to pass the 11+ examination, I found myself in the lowest grade at secondary modern school. One day Mrs Peel, my English teacher, spent five minutes talking with me. "You may never be good at examinations, but I have seen you play football," she said. "You give everything, you work hard and you inspire people. Keep going, because I believe you can do whatever you want in your life."

What concrete things did Mrs Peel do to encourage me?

- She set aside time to talk with me.
- She sat beside me, looked at me and asked me to listen to her.
- She told me what I did well and gave me specific examples.
- She told me I was already doing several things right, such as working hard and motivating other people.
- She told me that, providing I kept doing these things, I could do what I wanted in life.

Recalling how your Encouragers inspired you, how do you want to help other people? Describe your ideas on the page headed My Encouragement

MY ENCOURAGERS

THE PEOPLE WHO HAVE ENCOURAGED ME	THE SPECIFIC THINGS THEY DID TO ENCOURAGE ME
● _____	● _____ ● _____ ● _____
● _____	● _____ ● _____ ● _____
● _____	● _____ ● _____ ● _____

Plan. Write the names of three people you want to encourage. When do they come alive? How do you want to help them to use their talents? Write the specific things you can do to encourage each of these people.

You can give people hope

Virginia Satir inspired many people by pioneering family therapy in the 1950s. Troubled parents often failed to communicate clearly, she said, and this led to suffering. The "family pain" was then heaped on a "problem child" or another family scapegoat. How could she rekindle hope?

Virginia invited the parents to recall their first meeting by asking the husband: "Where did you meet your wife? What attracted you to her as a woman?" While the children listened, their father described the young woman he saw for the first time. She was so beautiful, so alive, so exciting. Hope flooded into the therapy room and Virginia could begin working with the family.

People want to be loved, but they often push away the very thing they want. Writing in *The Satir Model*, the authors recall that Virginia believed people often got into trouble because they had good intentions but poor communication. She looked beneath their difficult behaviour to find the real message they were trying to communicate. Virginia said: "When somebody would tell me that they were so angry they wanted to kill their mother, I would say: 'That says something to me about something you want from her. What is it? I would go off the killing and into the wanting.'"

All people have the right to believe in their own experience and picture of the world, said Virginia, but this is difficult in a troubled family. A person who is told what they *should* feel, see and hear begins to lose confidence. An abused son will become extremely disturbed when told he should love his abusing parents. So will the daughter who is told: "Keep working hard, but you will never be as good as your brother."

Virginia believed in what she called:

The Five Freedoms

The freedom to see and hear what is here, instead of what should be, was, or will be.

The freedom to say what you feel and think, instead of what you should.

MY ENCOURAGEMENT PLAN

Write the names of three people you want to encourage
and the specific things you want to do to encourage them.

THE PEOPLE I WANT TO ENCOURAGE	THE SPECIFIC THINGS I WANT TO DO TO ENCOURAGE THEM
● _____	● _____ ● _____ ● _____
● _____	● _____ ● _____ ● _____
● _____	● _____ ● _____ ● _____

The freedom to feel what you feel, instead of what you ought.

The freedom to ask for what you want, instead of always waiting for permission.

The freedom to take risks on your own behalf, instead of choosing to be only "secure" and not rocking the boat.

Born in Wisconsin in 1916, Virginia learned these lessons early in life. She describes her mother as a "genius" who turned cast-off garments into beautiful clothes. Her father was another "genius" who could look at a keyhole, go to the forge and immediately create a key that worked. Talking with Laurel King, author of *Women of Power*, she recalls that both parents had high standards of commitment. If you made a promise, you kept it. Her mother always looked for ways to improve things, saying: "Well, how can we fix it?"

Virginia adds: "Those years of my childhood really were very nice for me. I had the run of the farm and lots of pets. I loved them. Our chief babysitter was a large dog, a cross between a Newfoundland and a collie. My mother said she could never have brought us up without him."

Virginia was five when her world was shattered. Suffering appendicitis, she was refused medical care by her mother, a Christian Scientist. Her parents argued for three weeks over whether or not to take her to hospital. Peritonitis set in and the doctor pronounced her as good as dead. Virginia had great fighting spirit and spent several months in hospital willing herself back to life. She returned to a nightmare world where her previously loving parents behaved crazily. Her father burned her mother's religious books and she took revenge by cutting off her daughter's "gorgeous red wavy" hair. Shortly after that Virginia suffered an ear infection.

She adds: "It rendered me totally deaf within a matter of weeks. I did go back to school, and very few people knew I was deaf because I developed such a keen ability to observe people . . . I learned to lip-read, and I spelled out all the words because in those days they didn't have signs. I didn't have any professional help. I made up my own way of communicating with people because I wanted to connect with them, and that is true today. I make up whatever I need to do to talk with people who can't talk — the blind, the deaf, people of different languages."

Virginia was deaf for two years, had braces on her ankles and suffered failing eyesight. Seeing this as a challenge, she recalls: "I remember very

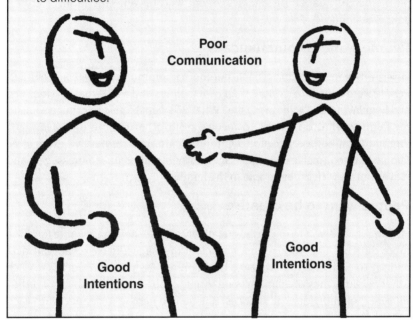

PEOPLE HAVE GOOD INTENTIONS

Virginia Satir believed that many people got into difficulties because they had good intentions but poor communication. She helped them to clarify what they wanted to say, to communicate clearly and to find positive solutions to difficulties.

Poor Communication

Good Intentions

Good Intentions

clearly when I was five years old, saying to myself, 'When I grow up I am going to be a children's detective of parents.' I had no idea what it would be, but it had to do with puzzles."

Twenty years later Virginia became her own kind of "detective": a psychiatric social worker helping troubled people. She rejected the route of studying pathology. Why? She felt that "Professionals" told people what they did wrong without offering solutions. Such methods were doomed to failure, so she adopted a different approach. According to the authors of *The Satir Model*, Virginia saw a person's symptoms as a cry for help:

"I saw this behaviour as saying to the world: 'Look, this seed is dying; it needs help' . . . I have found that if a person is in front of me they have strength because they're living and therefore I work with that strength."

Virginia started her own practice in 1951, taking high-risk patients and achieving excellent results. Patients sometimes relapsed when returning home, however, so she began treating whole families. She believed healthy families were those where people communicated clearly and were encouraged to grow as individuals. Troubled families were those where people lacked communication skills and stopped each other growing. Family problems got heaped on one scapegoat who became the family's cry for help. She believed:

People want to communicate

Virginia began by helping each person to communicate *within themselves*. People were invited to explore their own feelings and ask: "What do I feel, see and hear? What do I want in my life? What do I want to give to other people in my family? What do I want to receive from other people in my family?" Virginia then helped people to communicate and connect *with each other*. People learned to give clear messages, rather than confused messages, and make contact with other people in the family.

People want to be creative

Helping one person to develop is relatively simple; helping a whole family is more difficult. Everybody must give clear messages, make clear contracts and say to each other: "It's okay to be different." People are attracted to each other because they are similar, said Virginia, but they will only grow if they nurture their individual differences. She helped people to connect with each other but also grow as creative individuals. Virginia became known as the "Columbus" of family therapy, travelled the world running workshops and wrote a best-selling book called *The New Peoplemaking*. She died in 1988, but her wisdom will benefit many future generations.

Virginia Satir helped people to take charge of their lives. How can you be a good Encourager? Although you will behave differently in the family and at work, there are certain principles you can follow in many situations. Imagine one of your staff has requested a meeting with you to discuss his or her future. The next chart describes how to create a positive climate in the meeting. Many of these principles will be explored in greater depth later in the book.

THE ENCOURAGER'S GUIDE

How can you encourage a person? Imagine somebody at work has asked for a meeting to discuss his or her future. You can take the following steps towards creating a positive climate during the meeting.

1)   Welcome the person.

- Get "the first ten seconds" right.
- Make eye contact with them.
- Greet them in the appropriate manner.
- Arrange the seating in a way which will help you to communicate.
- Give your total attention to the person.
- Get the "social part" right before moving on to the main topic of the meeting. Offer the person coffee or do other things to help them to feel at ease.

2)   Agree on the goals for the meeting.

- Say what you see as the goals for the meeting.
- Ask what the person wants to get from the meeting.
- Make a "clear contract" about the goals and length of the meeting.

3)   Encourage the person to talk about themselves.

- Invite them to talk about the first subject on their agenda.
- Make sure you understand the person's picture of the world.
- Listen for the "headline" in what they are saying.
- Ask yourself: "How have I shown the person that I understood what they said?"

- Check out your understanding of what they mean by asking: "Are you saying that . . . .?" Look for the person responding by nodding or saying "Yes."

4) Encourage the person to set specific goals.

- Encourage them to take responsibility for shaping their future: to say "I . . . ." and to focus on what they can do, rather than talk about what they can't do.

- Encourage them to use the three key words for being creative: "What? How? When?" Ask them:

"What do you want to do?"

"How can you do it?"

"When do you want to begin?"

- Encourage them to make specific action plans for reaching their goals. Make sure they build in some early guaranteed successes.

- If appropriate, move on to exploring their strengths and areas for improvement.

5) Encourage the person to build on their strengths.

- Encourage them to develop their talents. Ask them:

"What do you see as your strengths? What do you do well? What are three things you have achieved during the last three months?"

"How do you want to build on your strengths?"

"When do you want to try?"

- Give examples of when you have seen them "come alive". Say what you saw them doing right then, and encourage them to follow these paths again in the future.

6)   Encourage the person to tackle any areas for improvement.

- If appropriate, ask the person: "What do you think you can do even better in the future? How can you do this?
  When do you want to try?"

- Encourage them to set specific goals for building on their strengths and tackling any areas for improvement.

7)   Finish the meeting in a positive way.

- Complete all the items on the agenda.

- Check they have covered everything they wanted to discuss and that they feel finished. If not, arrange another time to meet. Summarise any actions to be taken.

- Get the last ten seconds right and finish the meeting in a positive way.

You can offer people choices

Encouragers aim to increase people's repertoire of choices. The more choices people have, the more freedom they have to shape their future lives. Offering options is vital, but finally they must take responsibility for shaping their own futures. How can you give people this sense of ownership? One way is to invite them to tackle exercises which clarify their options. You may find it useful to do these exercises yourself, however, before using them to help other people.

**TEN THINGS I WANT
TO DO IN MY LIFE**

I want:

1. To keep myself healthy.

2. To keep encouraging my partner.

3. To make a living doing work I enjoy.

4. To help my children find satisfying work.

5. To . . . .

Etc.

MY IDEAL LIFE

would be:

1. To live with my family in the country.

2. To make my living by running my own carpentry business.

3. To make sure our children can learn in a small village school.

4. To encourage my partner to develop a career as a computer programmer.

5. To . . . .

Etc.

1)   Ten things I want to do in my life

Write a list of all your hopes and dreams. After completing your list, re-organise the items and place them in order of priority. Make concrete plans for doing one thing towards your first goal in the next week.

2)   My ideal life

Make a poster describing your ideal life. Then choose one small concrete step you can take towards reaching the easiest of these goals. Do something towards it during the next week.

3)   My future life

Draw a map showing the possible roads you can travel in the future. Let's explore how this works in practice.

Maria was a 17-year-old athlete who asked for help in considering her future. A county champion at 800 metres, she felt unsure as to whether or not to pursue her athletics career. She wanted to run for England, an ambition she had nursed since the age of eight, but now faced crucial decisions. Sports, college and her personal life were bunched together, creating conflicting demands.

"My inside feels like tangled spaghetti," she said. "I want to straighten things out." She began by tackling the exercise called My Future Life. Maria drew a map of the possible roads she could travel in the next six months, 18 months and three years. She also described the possible pluses and minuses of travelling each road.

Maria's first road was the most obvious. She could continue at college, pass her examinations, study sports psychology at university and continue her athletics career. Her second road started with passing her examinations but then took another route. She could take a year off, work as a volunteer at Camp America, travel to different countries and try a variety of jobs. Maria felt this would help her settle on her future career before studying for suitable professional qualifications.

Her third road also called for passing examinations but then took a radical turn. Maria had been offered a job at the local leisure centre. She could take the job, gain hands-on business experience and use the knowledge to start her own company. Athletics training had nurtured her

23

inner discipline and, being an independent type, she wanted to control her own destiny. Running a fitness centre appealed to her, but that would take years. Maria could begin by starting her own aerobics classes and developing a small part-time business. After completing her drawing, she listed the pluses and minuses of travelling each road.

Maria spent the next 30 minutes describing the different roads and the possible consequences. She was then invited to draw the road she really wanted to travel. How? She looked at her map, circled the best parts of each route and joined these parts together to create a new road.

Maria drew a fresh map of the road she aimed to travel in the next three years. She planned to pass examinations, focus on athletics, study sports psychology, do volunteer work at Camp America and take business studies as an extra option at university. Pluses: combining the best parts of each road; athletics, travel, helping people, sports psychology and business. Minuses: maintaining her inner-discipline, working hard and limiting her social life. Maria accepted the whole package of pluses and minuses. She then made specific plans for taking steps along her chosen road.

What kind of person can tackle this exercise? Maria was exceptional, but I have used it with people from all walks of life: teenagers, alcoholics, drug addicts, scientists and business directors. Some suggestions:

- Have high expectations. Whoever you invite to do the exercise, expect them to draw the possible roads they can follow.

- Be a good model. Before inviting people to draw their maps, give examples of the possible roads you can travel in your own life and work.

- Give people time and space to draw their maps. Make sure they understand the instructions, leave them alone and they will complete the drawing.

Encouragers help people to increase their repertoire of choices, which is also a key role played by teachers, so let's explore how to inspire people in education.

MY FUTURE LIFE

Make a map of the possible roads you can travel in the next six months, 18 months and three years. Add what you see as the possible pluses and minuses of following each road. Here, for example, is a map drawn by Maria, a 17-year-old county athletics champion.

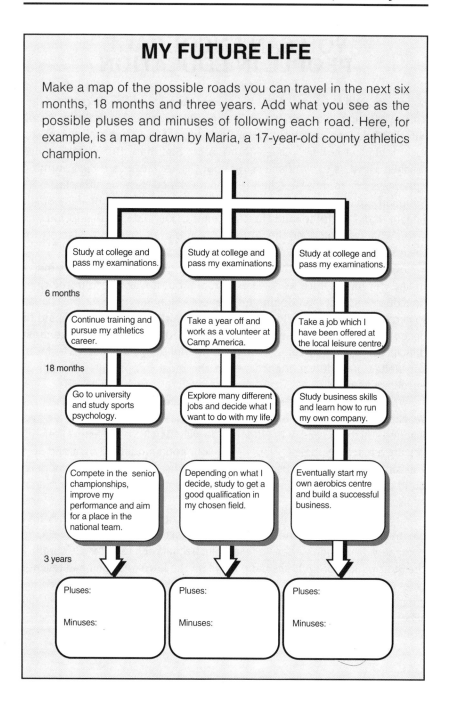

6 months

Study at college and pass my examinations.	Study at college and pass my examinations.	Study at college and pass my examinations.
Continue training and pursue my athletics career.	Take a year off and work as a volunteer at Camp America.	Take a job which I have been offered at the local leisure centre.

18 months

Go to university and study sports psychology.	Explore many different jobs and decide what I want to do with my life.	Study business skills and learn how to run my own company.
Compete in the senior championships, improve my performance and aim for a place in the national team.	Depending on what I decide, study to get a good qualification in my chosen field.	Eventually start my own aerobics centre and build a successful business.

3 years

Pluses: Minuses:	Pluses: Minuses:	Pluses: Minuses:

YOU CAN ENCOURAGE PEOPLE IN EDUCATION

Maybe I am old fashioned, but I believe teachers can change a person's life. Thirty years ago I was working nights on a factory machine in Derby. Along with my fellow engineering apprentices, I spent two days a month at the local technical college. One afternoon Mr Smitman, the social studies teacher, asked us to write an essay about George Orwell's 1984. Returning our essays one month later, he wrote on my paper: "See me after class." Mr Smitman explained that he taught GCE English at night school and thought I might find it useful to study for the examination. "I'd like to help you," he said. "Whatever you do in the future, I am sure you won't be in a factory for the rest of your life."

Two years later I left the assembly line to become a filing clerk in the Inland Revenue. Office work wasn't Utopia, but it was a step in the right direction. One year later Community Service Volunteers gave me the chance to care for mentally handicapped children. Thirty years later I am paid to encourage people because Mr Smitman helped me to take the first, most difficult step. Teachers can give many wonderful things to students — facts, knowledge and life experience — but the most important is the gift of encouragement.

Who have been your best teachers? Try the exercise called My Positive Teacher. Write the name of a person who passed on their knowledge and inspired you to succeed. What did they do well to help you to learn? Perhaps you are a teacher yourself. Clarify what your good model did right and how you can follow similar steps in your own teaching. Learn from your models, build on your strengths and inspire your students to reach their personal goals.

Great educators build good relationships with their students. They find creative ways to welcome students and make learning attractive. One secondary school in Sweden, for example, begins each term by "Celebrating the Start of School". A brass band plays on the lawn and the head teacher greets students at the gate. She directs them to the canteen, where cakes, ice cream and fruit are served. Students spend the first two days making the school look beautiful and meeting with teachers to set their personal goals.

MY POSITIVE TEACHER

1) Think of a teacher who encouraged and helped you to do your best. Write the name of the person.

- _____

2) What did they do well as a teacher? Write what you believe they did right in passing on their knowledge and helping you to succeed.

- _____
- _____
- _____
- _____
- _____

3) How can you follow these paths in your own way? Write three concrete things you can do to encourage other people in your work as an educator.

- _____
- _____
- _____

Great educators gain respect from their students. They are good models, enthusiastic and love their subject. They make learning interesting, say what they offer and make clear contracts with the students. Responsibility is a two-way street: so they expect students to work hard, develop their talents and improve their performance.

Recognising that students learn in different ways, they use different learning media. High expectations are vital. They expect students to be creative, to develop their natural talents and to make superb finished products. They make learning personal, practical and profitable, showing how students can apply the knowledge. Great educators follow the original Three Rs. They make learning real, relevant and rewarding.

YOU CAN MAKE LEARNING REAL

Sylvia Ashton-Warner was a remarkable teacher who worked with Maori children in New Zealand during the 1930s. Experts flocked to study her methods because she achieved outstanding results, helping the children to learn to read and write.

What was her secret? Sylvia believed in organic reading and writing. Learning must be real: it should start from a person's experience and relate to their world. Writing in her book *Teacher*, she stresses the need to balance such beliefs with hard work and discipline. "Discipline is a matter of being able to get attention when you want it," she says.

Calling the children to attention each morning by playing the first eight notes of Beethoven's Fifth Symphony, Sylvia asks the class to tackle their work. She calls each child to her in turn. "What word do you want today?" she asks Gay, the first child, who replies: "House." Sylvia writes the word on a piece of cardboard. She then asks Gay to trace the word with her finger and say it out loud. Gay "owns" the word, it comes from her guts. Sylvia makes sure that Gay says the word, sees the word and feels it in her body. She gives Gay the cardboard, asks her to keep her "word" for the day and repeats the process with each child. When class finishes Sylvia collects all the words on the pieces of cardboard.

Next morning Sylvia starts class by tipping the cardboard words on to the floor. "Find your word," she tells the children. Gay leaps from the chair and rummages in the pile. "House," she shouts, "I have found my word." She learned it by heart.

Children have two visions, an inner vision and an outer vision, says Sylvia, and it is the inner vision which burns brighter. Gay grasps the word which she spoke from her inner vision. Sylvia asks each child to choose a partner, speak their words and hear their partner's words. While the children teach each other, she repeats the process of inviting each child to choose their word for today. They build up what Sylvia calls their Key Vocabulary.

What happens if Gay fails to find her word? Sylvia rips up the piece of cardboard. The word has failed the "one look" test and cannot have any great meaning for Gay. Classrooms often display Jack and Jill illustrations for introducing the reading vocabulary to five-year-olds, says Sylvia, but it is a vocabulary chosen by educationalists in Auckland. Gay owns only those words that have come from deep within herself. She is more likely to love these words and want to write them on paper.

Sylvia helps the children to write by inviting them to draw pictures and add their own captions. They build up their words into sentences and create books about their experiences. Children write one word, then two sentences, then three, until six-year-olds are writing half a page a day and seven-year-olds a page or more a day. Sylvia continues:

"The drama of these writings could never be captured in a bought book. It could never be achieved in the most faithfully prepared teaching books. No one book could ever hold the variety of subjects that appears collectively in the infant room each morning. Moreover, it is written in the language that they use themselves. The books they write are the most dramatic and pathetic and colourful things I've ever seen on pages."

Shouldn't these Maori children be learning the Queen's English? Once they know the joy of creating their own words, says Sylvia, they reach out longingly to learn about other cultures. Reaching out for a book must become an organic action. She continues:

"Back to these first words. To these first books. They must be made out of the stuff of the child itself. I reach a hand into the mind of the child, bring out a handful of the stuff I find there, and use that as our first working material. Whether it is good or bad stuff, violent or placid stuff, coloured or dun . . . And in this dynamic material, within the familiarity and security of it, the Maori finds that words have intense meaning to him, from which cannot help but arise a love of reading. For it is here, right in this first word, that the love of reading is born, and the longer his reading is organic the stronger it becomes, until by the time he arrives at the books of the new culture, he receives them as another joy rather than as a labour."

Sylvia Ashton-Warner was highly successful, so opponents found it hard to argue with the results. Apart from making education real for the Maori children, she took the next step taken by many people who help students to develop their talents.

YOU CAN MAKE LEARNING RELEVANT

"But I don't work with children in New Zealand," somebody may say. "I educate managers in a company. How can I make learning relevant?" The same rules apply. People learn best when they see how they can use the knowledge today and tomorrow. Business managers want practical tools which they can use in their daily work. Imagine a group of managers have asked you to run a programme on developing leadership skills. Let's explore the steps you can take to make this or any other course relevant and rewarding.

CLARIFY THE GOALS FOR THE COURSE

Start from your destination and work backwards. Listen to your customers. Meet the managers and ask them: "What are the concrete results you want to achieve from the course?" Design the programme by integrating what they want to learn with what you want to offer, and then send a short course description to the managers. For example:

DEVELOPING LEADERSHIP SKILLS

This two-day course will provide managers with a framework and practical tools which they can use

- To provide good leadership.
- To build on their strengths as leaders.
- To develop coaching skills.
- To encourage people to do their best.
- To build successful teams.

The course will be enjoyable but hard work. Managers will take away practical ideas and tools which they can use in their daily work.

MAKE AN OVERALL ROAD MAP FOR THE COURSE

Draw a map which shows the topics you aim to cover during the two days. Brainstorm all the themes you want to include in the programme. Break these down into manageable chunks, ensure the programme has a logical flow and put all this information on a large paper. Your map for the two-day programme may look something like that shown on the next page.

Keep in touch with your customers. After completing your outline, check with the managers that the content meets their needs. Describe the themes to be covered, then ask: "Is there anything you would like to add or change?" Alter the programme to match their agenda.

YOU CAN MAKE LEARNING REWARDING

Great educators go beyond teaching theory. They often introduce some form of "learning by doing" in their lessons. Why? People learn in different ways: some learn by listening, others learn by seeing, feeling, talking, reading, thinking, reflecting, acting, writing, drawing and creating. How can you reach the managers who have different learning styles?

PROGRAMME TITLE

FIRST DAY

Introduction
Goals for the programme

1. _____
2. _____
3. _____
4. _____
5. _____

● How to provide good leadership

* _____
* _____
* _____

Coffee

● How to build on your strengths as a leader

* _____
* _____
* _____

Lunch

● How to develop coaching skills

* _____
* _____
* _____

Tea

* _____
* _____

Close

SECOND DAY

Introduction to the day

Review of the previous day

Goals for the second day

● How to encourage people to do their best

* _____
* _____

Coffee

● How to build a successful team

* _____
* _____
* _____

Lunch

● How to apply the learning in your daily work

* _____
* _____
* _____

Tea

● How to get some early successes

Action planning/conclusion

FOLLOW THE "ONE-TWO-THREE" MODEL FOR RUNNING THE COURSE

Begin the course by winning and inspiring the managers. Show that you understand their world and the challenges they face in the company. Introduce the first theme and follow the "One-Two-Three" model for helping people to learn. (See next page.)

STEP ONE: INTRODUCE THE THEME

For example: Show what good leaders do right to achieve superb results. Show people what works, rather than what fails. Give colourful examples and highlight success stories from business, the arts, sports and other walks of life.

STEP TWO: GIVE AN ACTIVITY ON THE THEME

For example: Invite people to tackle an exercise called My Positive Leader. This is an old exercise, but it will also act as an ice-breaker. Invite each person to write the name of a good leader they have known. Ask them to identify five things that leader did right to achieve positive results. Finally, ask people to form groups, share their lists and create a composite poster which shows the qualities demonstrated by good leaders.

STEP THREE: SUM UP THE THEME

For example: Give each group five minutes to present their poster to the other managers. Giving people the chance to present finished products — such as posters, sketches or solutions to problems — encourages them to share their know-how and feel successful. Share your own knowledge by describing practical tools the managers can use to provide good leadership in their daily work. Conclude the session by making a link to the next theme and repeat the "One-Two-Three" model throughout the course.

RUNNING THE COURSE

You can run the course by following the "One-Two-Three" model for helping people to learn

- Begin the session
- Win and inspire people in your own way

STEP ONE: INTRODUCE THE THEME

- Give people a short introduction to the theme
- Give people lots of colourful examples
- Give people positive models and examples

STEP TWO: GIVE AN ACTIVITY ON THE THEME

- Give people some learning-by-doing
- Give people chance to "own" the knowledge
- Give people chance to use their energy in a positive way
- Give people a practical exercise, role-play, etc.
- Give people chance to produce some finished product

STEP THREE: SUM UP THE THEME

- Give people chance to present their conclusions
- Give people chance to clarify what they have learned
- Give people practical tools or something else of take-home value
- Link to the next theme and repeat the "One-Two-Three" model

MAKE THE LEARNING ENJOYABLE AND EFFECTIVE

Complete your preparations for the course by making a detailed plan for each session. Find creative ways to bring the learning to life. Taking each theme in turn, use the three keywords: "What? How? When?" Ask yourself:

a)   What do I want to help people to learn?

For example: Exploring the third theme on the course, you may say: "I want to help the managers to develop their coaching skills." Why? Managers will then be more likely to encourage their people to perform quality work for the company. How can you bring this theme to life? Ask yourself:

b)   How can I help people to learn this in an enjoyable and effective way?

Brainstorm ideas for helping the managers to develop their coaching skills. Start with the words: "I can . . . ." and produce lots of ideas. Go for quantity first, then go for quality. When brainstorming, remember the different kinds of activities you can use to bring the learning to life. These include:

- Lectures
- Theories and models
- Learning by doing
- Pairs exercises
- Whole group exercises
- Role-plays
- Simulations
- Group discussions
- Quizzes
- Self-evaluation exercises
- Card sorts
- Success stories
- Pen and paper exercises
- Individual exercises
- Small group exercises
- Posters
- Sketches
- Tackling real-life issues
- Teaching each other
- Videos
- Case studies
- Etc.

Decide on the ideas you will use to develop the managers' coaching skills; then finalise your plans for running the session. Repeat this process throughout the programme. Finally, ask yourself:

c)   When do I want to offer this learning to people?

Return to your overall road map for the course. Do the two days have a logical flow? What can be improved? Finalise the programme, write the course materials and fix practical things at the course venue. The next step is to run the course for the managers.

Good education is like good design. It is vital to complete the job successfully but also give people space to find their own truth. Many of us recall teachers who signposted the way to a better world. While honouring these teachers, we recognise that we must take responsibility for developing our own talents. Many of us find such fulfilment by performing satisfying work, which highlights the next step taken by Encouragers.

YOU CAN ENCOURAGE PEOPLE IN WORK

Richard Bolles has helped literally thousands of people to find their real work in life. *What Colour Is Your Parachute?* was first published in 1970. Since then this inspiring book has been reprinted more than twenty times and is updated annually. Twenty-five-thousand people a month buy the book, which has sold well over four million copies. Packed with cartoons and practical exercises which bring the book to life, it has drawn praise from job-seekers and career counsellors. The *Mississippi Business Journal* wrote, for example:

"Richard Bolles created this classic 20 years ago, and he updates it annually . . . The sheer force of this book is hard to fathom . . . No other book can do so much for job-hunters and career-changers . . . So take the advice of myself and others and read this classic, because they don't get any better. Bolles knows his subject supremely . . . "

What is the secret of *Parachute*? Richard combines down-to-earth advice to job-seekers with an invitation to follow their life-mission. He asks questions such as: "What do you enjoy doing? What are your transferable skills? What do you want to leave behind on Earth?" The questions are accompanied by practical exercises and suggestions which help people to find their vocation.

How can you help a person who asks: "What job should I do in my life?" Begin by inviting them to do the exercises in Richard's book or ask them, for example, to write a list headed "Thirty things I enjoy doing". Brainstorm how they can make money doing some of these things. Expand on this theme by looking at how they can earn a living doing what they love. You can also ask them to do the exercise on the next page called Mission and Mortgage.

"How long will it take me to change my life?" is a question posed by many people. Some people can change their lives tomorrow, but they may also want to retain their financial status. How long will it take them to get the right balance between pursuing their mission and paying their mortgage? Probably three years, providing they are willing to work hard and make some changes in life-style. Sounds a long time? The alternative is to live for 70 years without pursuing one's vocation. People in the richer nations are lucky to have this choice. Not everybody is so fortunate. Innovative people in poorer countries have much to teach us, however, and provide inspiring lessons for those who seek to pursue their life mission.

YOU CAN HELP PEOPLE TO DO POSITIVE WORK

Ashoka is a charitable organisation which gives financial backing to public entrepreneurs in the Third World. What is a public entrepreneur? Somebody with an innovative idea which will improve people's quality of life. This might be in the field of, for example, human rights, medical care, education, agriculture, housing or broadcasting. Ashoka looks for individuals who have the passion and practical skills to implement their vision.

"What differentiates Ashoka Fellows from mere idealists," says William Drayton, the organisation's founder, "is that for these rare men and women, an idea can bring satisfaction only when it is realised. Possessing the same unstoppable drive of a Steve Jobs (co-founder of Apple Computers), they define new issues and create new approaches. Their innovations then set new yardsticks of performance for helping society."

Ashoka finances people whose ideas can have far-reaching impact. It will support new teaching methods which can spread across a nation, but will not set up a new school. It will support initiatives which empower people to take care of their health, but will not finance a clinic. A non-profit organisation independent from any government or religious affiliation, Ashoka provides the "Fellows" with their basic living costs of, for example, £400 per month over a one to four-year period. This support buys people the time to implement their ideas. By 1994 Ashoka had financed some 500 public entrepreneurs in South America, Asia and Africa. People mentioned in the foundation's Eleventh Year Report include:

MISSION AND MORTGAGE

Write down: a) The things you can do to pursue your mission.

b) The things you can do to pay your mortgage.

c) The things you can do to get the right balance between pursuing your mission and paying your mortgage.

HOW I CAN PURSUE MY MISSION

- _____
- _____
- _____

HOW I CAN PAY MY MORTGAGE

- _____
- _____
- _____

HOW I CAN GET THE RIGHT BALANCE BETWEEN PURSUING MY MISSION AND PAYING MY MORTGAGE

- _____
- _____
- _____

● Osman Gani, Bangladesh

Osman helps thousands of small farmers whose land disappears as river channels shift in Bangladesh. He organises and helps them to find allies in both government and the law. Instead of losing all their assets to rich and powerful landowners, the farmers are assisted to find new land and rebuild their lives.

● Maria José de Faria, Brazil

When Maria gave birth to a Down's Syndrome child she experienced the prejudice which surrounds such children and their families. Poor people face special difficulties when caring for the children, so she began by building a support group for their parents. Maria has since gone on to provide practical information and education to millions of people by broadcasting programmes on radio and TV in Brazil.

● Inderjit Khurana, India

Founder of a large private school, Inderjit wondered how the children who begged on railway stations could get a good education. Her solution was to bring schools to the platforms. She combines imaginative teaching methods with offering the children medical aid, counselling and job training. Inderjit is now negotiating with Indian Railways to expand platform schools across the country.

● Mario Ottoboni, Brazil

A spiritually committed lawyer, he gave up his practice to show how prisoners could be rehabilitated. Mario's methods include treating the prisoners with respect, getting them to serve as guards and gradually re-introducing them to the community. Eighty per cent of Brazil's prisoners normally re-offend; ninety-six per cent of prisoners who have attended Mario's programme have not returned to prison.

● Carlos Roberto dos Santos, Brazil

Orphaned as a child, Carlos spent some time living on the streets. Now a sergeant in the Brazilian Air Force, he has shown how the military can use its facilities to give street children pride, education and the credibility to get a decent job. Carlos is spreading this model for helping children throughout the military and inside the police force.

● Rajesh Shrestha, Nepal

Eighty per cent of Nepal's rural population live in sub-standard housing. Rajesh, an architect, is developing alternative building techniques which can be used by the poor. His methods are based on using durable local materials, such as mud and bamboo, which provide good housing and maintain the integrity of traditional building styles.

Ashoka has four criteria for selecting a Fellow:

1) They must be innovative.
2) They must have entrepreneurial skills.
3) They must be able to make a far-reaching impact.
4) They must have great personal integrity.

How successful are the public entrepreneurs? A large proportion of them have had either a regional, state or national impact. Why? Ashoka takes great care in selecting its Fellows. Apart from providing them with their basic living costs, it offers the gathered wisdom of its members by putting them in touch with other innovators. It also has an "Entrepreneur to Entrepreneur" programme, linking leading business entrepreneurs with the Fellows. Individuals can do quality work, but sometimes change calls for people working well together, so let's explore how to create good teams.

YOU CAN HELP PEOPLE TO BUILD POSITIVE TEAMS

Imagine you are employed as a consultant to the White House, a treatment centre for 40 troubled teenagers. Derek, the Community Director, is worried about staff morale and has asked you to run six sessions on team building. How can you help the eight youth workers to combine their talents?

You may wish to start by clarifying your own philosophy about successful teamwork. Try tackling the exercise on the next page called The Positive Team. Recall a team you have enjoyed being part of in sports, the arts, business or any walk of life. Describe what people did right to work well together and how you can help the staff to follow similar steps at the White House.

Clear contracting is also vital. Ask Derek: "What are three concrete results you want to achieve by holding the team building programme?" Encouragers can offer people practical tools that work. They cannot change individuals or perform miracles. Describe what you can and cannot offer the staff. Derek must still make leadership decisions about who stays and who leaves the team. Conclude the discussion by making a clear contract about your work at the White House.

Time to run the programme. The content of the sessions will be shaped by what you believe the youth workers must do to help the troubled teenagers. Building on your own philosophy, you may wish to bear several points in mind. People often take five steps towards building a good team.

THE POSITIVE TEAM

1) Write the name of a team which you have enjoyed being part of some time during your life. This can be a team in sports, music, theatre, work or any kind of team.

● _____

2) What did people do right to make it enjoyable and successful? Write down five things you believe they did right to build a good team.

● They _____

● They _____

● They _____

● They _____

● They _____

3) How can you encourage people to follow these steps in their own way to build good teams? Write three concrete things you can do to encourage people to work well together.

● I can _____

● I can _____

● I can _____

THE POSITIVE TEAM

People often take five steps towards building a good team. It is the leader's job to ensure that people follow these steps successfully:

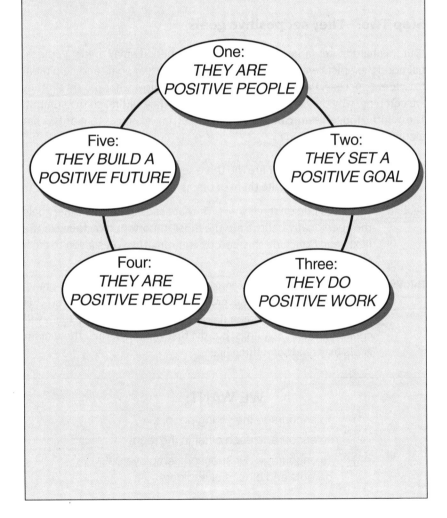

One:
*THEY ARE
POSITIVE PEOPLE*

Two:
*THEY SET A
POSITIVE GOAL*

Three:
*THEY DO
POSITIVE WORK*

Four:
*THEY ARE
POSITIVE PEOPLE*

Five:
*THEY BUILD A
POSITIVE FUTURE*

Step One: They are positive people

The White House staff need to have a positive attitude. Counselling troubled teenagers is a rewarding but challenging task, so all eight people must be pursuing their vocation. Derek cannot "persuade" people to change. They must choose to play a creative role. The White House team cannot afford the luxury of paying one person who is negative. Sounds tough, but teamwork calls for following certain rules. Superb teams employ people who provide energy, enthusiasm and encouragement.

Step Two: They set positive goals

"But it is hard to set targets in social work," somebody may argue. Perhaps, but good therapists encourage their clients to set clear goals and help them to achieve success. People work best when they know what mountain they are climbing, why they are climbing it and when they will reach the summit. The White House team can tackle a goal-setting exercise to clarify what mountain they are climbing.

First: Ask the staff: "What are the three key goals you want to achieve in the next year?" Invite them to brainstorm at least 25 ideas.

Second: Give each person three votes. They are each to tick the three goals they personally believe are the most important to achieve in the next year. Conclude this part by counting the votes given to each suggestion.

Third: Give the team 30 minutes to agree on their three main goals. Looking at the voting, several groupings will stand out, so this process will be easier than it sounds. The White House team will create their own headings, but the first version of their three main goals may read something like:

WE WANT:

1)   To encourage the young people.

2)   To encourage each other in the team.

3)   To encourage our sponsors: employers, parents and other stakeholders.

Set the team some homework to complete in the next week. People are to finalise the goals, also adding any sub-goals, to make the targets specific. Staff can present the final version to you at the next meeting. Finally, ask them to design a poster showing their team goals. They can display the poster in the staff room to remind themselves of their role at The White House. (This goal-setting exercise is explained in detail in *The Positive Planet**).

Step Three: They do positive work

The White House staff are lucky: they are paid to do work they enjoy. Encourage them to fulfil their purpose. They are hired to help the teenagers, rather than become paralysed looking inward. Inspire the staff to focus on how they can help the young people:

- To take responsibility for shaping their future.

- To build on their strengths.

- To set clear goals.

- To find or create work they love.

- To reach their goals.

The White House team must support each other and perform quality work. Superb service, not extensive self-analysis, will pay the mortgage, which highlights the next step taken by good teams.

Step Four: They get positive results

"But it is difficult to show what we achieve in social work," somebody may argue. "It is hard to convince the public that we offer value for money." Perhaps, but The White House team can strive to satisfy the people who pay their wages. How can they "make the invisible visible"? Derek can start weekly staff meetings by asking each person to write a list headed "Our Successes: Three things the young people have achieved in the last week". These can be individual or collective achievements. Staff can catalogue these tangible results in their annual report to parents, politicians and other stakeholders. The White House will then show it is fulfilling its purpose and helping the teenagers.

*By Mike Pegg, published by Enhance Ltd,

Step Five: They build a positive future

The White House team can be proactive. They can choose to make things happen, rather than let things happen. Staff can start by identifying the challenges they will face in the next three years, such as: higher truancy rates, cuts in funding and continued unemployment. The next step is to create specific strategies for tackling these challenges. Derek's team can also learn from their "customers". They can ask the teenagers, parents, politicians and other sponsors: "What do we do well? What can we do even better — and how?" Staff can then build on their strengths and introduce suggested improvements. The White House team can create a positive future.

E.F. Schumacher believed that small is beautiful, because individuals work best in small groups where they feel able to shape their destiny. People must sometimes work in larger organisations, however, which highlights another step taken by Encouragers.

YOU CAN HELP PEOPLE TO BUILD POSITIVE ORGANISATIONS

Sports Hotels* hires motivated people who aim to please customers and make money. Employees queue to work for the leisure group, which runs five activity centres in northern England. Despite the recession, the company has boosted its profits over the last five years. Why? First: People are becoming more health-conscious. They enjoy the wide range of activities the company offers: health checks, aerobics, canoeing, rock climbing, etc. Second: Staff provide excellent customer service. Third: The company is crystal clear about how it runs its business.

"Belief is vital in our business, so we hire enthusiastic people who believe in what we offer the market," says Lynn, the managing director. "We run a simple business and aim to keep it simple. Employees must want to give good service and make sure customers return to Sports Hotels." Lynn's senior management team has built a successful company by focusing on clarity, coaching and creativity.

CLARITY

Sports Hotels has clear goals. "We focus on our customers, colleagues and cash," says Lynn. "Senior managers communicate the company's goals. Then

*The name has been changed: but all the events took place in an actual hotel and leisure company.

each employee clarifies their part in achieving these goals." The company isn't a debating society, however, neither does it re-invent itself each year. Managers provide "Empowerment within Parameters". Staff are given clear guidelines as to what they can and cannot influence in their work. People then make clear contracts about their contribution to Sports Hotels.

Clarity is crucial in any kind of teamwork. If you wish, try tackling the exercise called The Thirty Seconds Test. Imagine you are travelling in a lift with a stranger. Seeing you are wearing a badge bearing the name of your organisation, he says: "I notice you work for . . . Could you tell me the goals of your organisation and your part in helping to achieve these goals?" You have 30 seconds to give your reply. Try this exercise with your colleagues to see if they give the same answer about the organisation's goals.

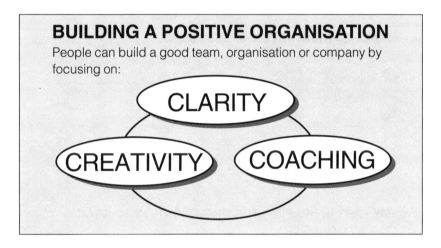

BUILDING A POSITIVE ORGANISATION

People can build a good team, organisation or company by focusing on:

CLARITY

CREATIVITY   COACHING

COACHING

"Our managers try to be coaches rather than cops," says Lynn. "They are answerable for the results, but they seldom do the work. We stand or fall by the quality of our staff. Our task is to coach and help the staff to serve the customers." Managers have three main tasks in Sports Hotels.

a) Managers must ensure their staff reach their agreed goals.

First: The manager meets the team to agree on their collective goals for the year. They follow up by holding weekly team meetings to review progress. People share successes, tackle areas for improvement and agree future action plans.

THE THIRTY SECONDS TEST

Imagine you are travelling in a lift with somebody you do not know. He notices you are wearing a badge which gives the name of your organisation. He says: "I see you work for . . . Could you tell me the goals of your organisation and your part in helping it to achieve these goals?" You have thirty seconds to answer.

MY ORGANISATION'S GOALS ARE:

- _____

- _____

- _____

MY PART IN HELPING THE ORGANISATION TO REACH THESE GOALS IS:

- _____

- _____

- _____

Second: The manager meets each person to agree on their individual goals for the year. They follow up by holding monthly meetings to review progress and agree goals for the next month. Ownership is vital, so the people clarify and write their own goals. What if they fail to reach their targets? The manager is "tough on the facts, but open on the reasons". Lessons are learned and applied when setting the next month's targets. Sounds exhausting, but regular meetings keep individuals on track.

b) Managers must ensure their staff do good quality work.

First: "Our managers are like football coaches. They must give players the support needed to do the job," says Lynn. "You cannot tell a football team to play without boots. Our staff must be given the practical help they need to give good service to the customers."

Second: The manager encourages people to build on their strengths and tackle areas for improvement. Before each monthly meeting, the person writes down:

Three successes I have achieved in the past month

- _____
- _____
- _____

Two things I can do even better in the next month

- _____
- _____

How to develop the person's talents? The manager spends at least 15 minutes clarifying what the employee did right to achieve the successes. "Keep doing what works," is common sense advice in most walks of life, so the person plans how to pursue similar steps in the next month. Tackling areas for improvement calls for asking: "What can you do even better next month?" Troubling situations may call for taking a tougher line. If the employee fails to suggest his or her own positive alternative, the manager gives clear messages about how he or she will be expected to behave in the future.

c) Managers must ensure their staff build high-quality self-
   managing teams.

"Sports Hotels would make money if I stayed in bed tomorrow," says Lynn. "But the business would fall apart if the staff failed to arrive in the morning. Breakfast would be locked in the kitchen, telephones would ring and the gym would be chaotic. Bad managers often prevent staff giving service to the customers, but good managers have a role to play. They can pass on their knowledge, educate people to see the big picture and coach them to manage themselves."

Millions of work teams function by themselves everyday, but sometimes they face internal disputes and become a collection of individuals pursuing their own agendas. How can they perform high quality work over a long period of time? The manager can start the ball rolling by asking them: "What can you do to become a self-managing team? What support and skills do you need? How can I help you to develop into a self-managing team over the next weeks, months and year?" Good coaches recognise that the best teams in sport, or any walk of life, consistently do high quality work by themselves.

CREATIVITY

"Sports Hotels depends on staff performing thousands of creative acts every day," says Lynn. "The receptionist offers to book a train ticket for a guest; the chef cooks a special meal for a vegetarian; the swimming coach finds new ways to teach a frightened 40-year-old how to swim."

Clarity gives birth to creativity. People who know the limits, what they can and cannot influence, will be inventive within these parameters. Sports Hotels' staff know the borders within which they can take risks. Standards are maintained by doing the right things in the right way every day, but they also have autonomy to please the customers. Good organisations focus on clarity, coaching and creativity. This generates a climate which inspires staff to use their talents.

Encouragers equip people to do good work as individuals, in teams and in organisations. Some people also expand their horizons beyond national borders.

YOU CAN ENCOURAGE
PEOPLE ACROSS THE PLANET

Elisabeth Kübler-Ross attracted both praise and criticism during her life. Swiss-born, she qualified as a doctor and emigrated to the United States. One day a hospital asked her to give a lecture on death and dying. Abandoning the traditional practice of reading notes from behind a lectern, she invited a dying woman to share the platform and talk about her feelings. Elisabeth's meeting attracted national attention and she was invited to run similar sessions across the country.

She embarked on a series of week-long workshops for mixed groups: people who were dying and people who were caring for the dying. "Helpers" learned from patients and, by coming to terms with their own deaths, people learned to live more fully. Elisabeth published her book *On Death and Dying* and travelled across the globe. Newspapers, magazines and the broadcasting media ran stories about her mission. She made mistakes in the following years (she once publicly backed a man who proved to be a criminal) but also helped thousands of people across the world. During the 1980s she turned to caring for children and adults suffering from AIDS.

Elisabeth saw the illness as a crucial test for humanity. In her book AIDS: *The Ultimate Challenge*, she describes how the epidemic gives each of us the opportunity to show our unconditional love. "We have to choose between rejecting millions of our own because of their illness," she said, "or reaching out to offer help, warmth and acceptance . . . It is our choice to live up to this ultimate challenge or to perish." Elisabeth believed humanity would shape its own future by the way it responded to people with AIDS.

" . . . We can destroy ourselves with our own self-imposed fears, blame, shame, negativity. We can become very vulnerable to diseases, and more panicky when the number of AIDS patients reaches a million and more. Or we can make our choices based on love and begin to heal, begin to serve those with AIDS and other diseases, to show compassion and understanding, and finally, before it is too late, to learn the final lesson, the lesson of unconditional love.

"AIDS poses its own threat to mankind, but unlike war, it is a battle from within, knowing no borders or national boundaries. Are we going to choose hate and discrimination, or will we have the courage to choose love and service? Yes, I truly believe that AIDS is the ultimate challenge for all of us . . . "

People choose different ways to climb a mountain. They also choose different ways to build a better world. Elisabeth's mission wove together three themes pursued by many caring people: they focus on health, hope and happiness.

They focus on health

They work for the health of people and the planet. They focus on offering people the basic materials of life: peace, health, food, housing and a clean environment.

They focus on hope

They work for human rights and hope. They focus on offering people freedom satisfying work and fair wages. Encouragers also believe in empowerment. They offer people practical tools which they can use to shape their own futures.

They focus on happiness

They recognise that many of the things that people aspire to — such as money, status and material goods — are seen as the keys to happiness. People must be given the basic materials for life, but they must also beware of chasing false gods. Encouragers help people to find ways to take charge of their own happiness.

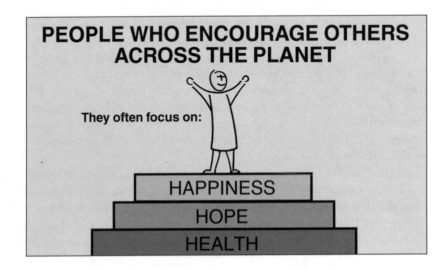

PEOPLE WHO ENCOURAGE OTHERS ACROSS THE PLANET

They often focus on:

HAPPINESS

HOPE

HEALTH

YOU CAN FOCUS ON HEALTH

Bernie Siegel has empowered thousands of cancer patients to improve the quality of their lives. An American surgeon, his best selling books, such as *Love, Medicine & Miracles* and *Peace, Love & Healing*, have touched readers around the world. In 1978 he founded ECaP, Exceptional Cancer Patients, groups of people determined to shape their future lives. Doctors quickly recognise patients who have read Bernie's books. Why? When entering hospital, such people make their conditions plain:

- They take an active role and refuse to be passive. They say things like: "This is my body and I have the right to decide what I want to do with it."

- They arrive in practical, comfortable clothes and plan to do lots of walking, rather than lie in bed.

- They insist on having a room with a view of the sky and the outside world. They steadfastly refuse to accept a room that faces a brick wall.

- They bring personal and inspiring decorations to put up in their room. They also bring a tape-recorder, tapes and headphones. Apart from playing their favourite music, they also record conversations with doctors.

- They continually question why tests or other procedures should take place. They insist on being told how a particular treatment is going to equip them to help themselves.

- They ask for their favourite music to be played in the operating room.

- They ask the surgeon to repeat positive messages to them during the operation. For example: "You will wake up comfortable, thirsty and hungry." If this is not possible, the surgical team is absolutely to avoid saying anything negative. Why? The patient's vulnerable body is open and sensitive to all outside influences.

- They start moving as soon as possible after surgery, leaving the hospital to attend group meetings, go for walks or have meals out with friends.

Bernie has suffered setbacks in his mission to empower patients. Inspired by the Simontons' pioneering visualisation work in the 1970s, he invited hundreds of patients to an evening meeting to hear about the new treatment. Expecting crowds of patients, relatives and friends to attend, he was surprised to find that only twelve people turned up on the night. Why? Bernie reluctantly faced the facts about people suffering from illness. He believes that:

- Between 15 and 20 per cent of patients are prepared to take responsibility for healing themselves. They are exceptional patients.

- Between 60 and 70 per cent of patients will perform to satisfy the doctor. They will be "good patients" and do what they are told.

- Between 15 and 20 per cent of patients unconsciously or consciously wish to die. As a caring person, Bernie found this part the hardest to accept.

What makes an exceptional patient? They keep their power, says Bernie. They have what psychologists call *an inner locus of control*. They know that happiness is an inside job. What is the role of the doctor? "My first job is to buy people time," says Bernie. Time gives them a chance to appreciate life and understand why they became sick. People can then experience true healing, not merely the reversal of disease. Healing doesn't always mean living longer, says Bernie. It does mean finding inner peace. He adds that recovery from illness depends on the "four faiths" — faith in oneself; faith in one's doctor; faith in one's treatment; faith in one's spiritual life. Bernie has equipped many people to follow this path and find their own personal peace.

YOU CAN FOCUS ON HOPE

"Without hope, the soul will perish," says the Bible. People choose different ways to offer others hope. Chad Varah created the Samaritans, which helps people who are contemplating suicide. Rosa Parks refused to give up her seat on a bus to a white man in Montgomery, Alabama. She fanned the flames of resistance and the torch was picked up by Martin Luther King. People must have hope and feel that life can be better.

How can you offer people hope? One way is to guide people through the stages of Inspiration, Implementation and Integration. Stage One is Inspiration: People need positive models who show that they can stand up for their rights and create a better life. Stage Two is Implementation: People need practical implementation tools which they can use to take charge of their lives and work. Stage Three is Integration: People need to integrate the learning into their daily lives and work to achieve ongoing success. The first step is to light the fires of hope, as one group of women, known as The Mothers, did in South America.

The Mothers gather at the Plaza de Mayo in the centre of Buenos Aires every Thursday afternoon. Fastening white head scarves around their heads, they silently walk in a circle around the monument of Independence. "Return Our Children Alive," is embroidered on their head scarves and they want information about their missing children. The women have been gathering every week since 1977. Argentina was then suffering under a military dictatorship which regularly practised detention, torture and murder. Jo Fisher describes the early days of the Mothers of the Disappeared in her book *Out Of The Shadows*.

"Every Thursday afternoon women began to gather silently in Plaza de Mayo. They sat on benches, identifying each other by a leaf pinned to their lapels or a flower in their hands, secretly passing each other messages. The penalty for illicit association was up to 25 years in prison and the Plaza de Mayo, opposite the presidential palace and historically the site of political and trade union demonstrations, was one of the most heavily guarded areas in Buenos Aires.

"By meeting in the square they were ignoring the advice of human rights organisations already in existence which discouraged illegal forms of action. They also ignored the government officials who warned that joining the women in the square would cost them all hope of ever seeing their children again. As mothers, they felt a special responsibility for finding their children and a desperation that they believed only other mothers could understand."

The Mothers issued the first public challenge to the military, writes Jo Fisher, who fell victim to their own prejudices about women. The military had silenced students, the church and opposition politicians. Surely they could not be threatened by middle-aged housewives? The Mothers were dismissed as "mad women" and given breathing space to organise. Sewing clubs, fashion shows and birthday parties became the cover for their challenge to military rule. Hebe, one of the Mothers, takes up the story in *Out of the Shadows*:

"We had to educate ourselves. The majority of us had hardly been to school. This is a macho country; we were used to talking about dress patterns and cooking, while the men discussed politics and football in another room. Women like us lived in an isolated world which finished at the front doors of our houses."

Television pictures of the Mothers flashed across the globe and the military junta became nervous, calling them "mothers of terrorists". The 1978 Soccer World Cup was intended to be a showpiece event which legitimised military rule in the eyes of the world. The junta was shocked when the Dutch football team, one of the favourites for the competition, chose to visit the Mothers rather than attend the expensive opening ceremony. Branding the women as political extremists proved fruitless, because they disowned all parties.

The Mothers embraced a different ethic, declaring: "We are life." Jane Jaquette, editor of *The Women's Movement In Latin America*, quotes one woman as saying: "No mother is asked what her ideology is or what she does; neither do we ask what her children were doing. We don't defend ideologies; we defend life." Maria del Carmen Feijoo underlines this philosophy in the same book. She writes:

"It was women who erected the principle of 'life' against a government which dismissed the value of human life. It was women who aroused a society that had become a silent accomplice in the face of these horrors . . . The paradigm of the Madres' politics was based on the all-out defence of the most basic principles — the defence of life and of the right to love. It unintentionally became a new feminist paradigm, sustaining the need for a feminine perspective in the world of patriarchal and masculine politics, and suggesting a broader vision capable of destroying the traditional rule of the political game."

The Mothers continued their protests and were joined by the Grandmothers, women whose daughters gave birth to children in concentration camps. The South Atlantic War eventually toppled the military junta and democracy was restored. Many women felt human rights to be the central issue of the election and supported politicians who promised to put the military junta on trial. They wanted the new Argentina to be based on justice, not revenge.

Ten years of broken promises has increased their scepticism about politicians while some of the Mothers and Grandmothers still search for their children. The pain remains, but the women have achieved much since that first Thursday in 1977. Lighting the flame of hope, they inspired thousands of others to fight injustice. As Maria Del Rosario, another of the Mothers, says:

"The square is our citadel. We'll only stop going to the square the day we're all dead, and not even then, because now Mothers are dying and they ask for their ashes to be scattered there."

YOU CAN FOCUS ON HAPPINESS

"Aristotle concluded that, more than anything else, men and women seek happiness," writes Mihaly Csikszentmihalyi in his book *Flow*. "While happiness is sought for its own sake, every other goal — health, beauty, money, or power — is valued only because we expect that it will make us happy."

Mihaly's book explores people's experiences of feeling fully alive. Beginning by asking artists, musicians and surgeons to describe their flow experiences, he then interviewed people from all walks of life, such as factory workers in Chicago, farmers in Italy and teenagers in Tokyo. "What I 'discovered' was that happiness is not something that just happens," writes Mihaly.

"We have all experienced times when, instead of being buffeted by anonymous forces, we do feel in control of our actions, masters of our own fate. On the rare occasions that it happens, we feel a sense of exhilaration, a deep sense of enjoyment that is long cherished and that becomes a landmark in memory for what life should be like . . . The best moments usually occur when a person's body or mind is stretched to its limits in a voluntary effort to accomplish something difficult and worthwhile. Optimal experience is therefore something that we *make* happen."

Mihaly's world-wide study says that people enjoy a sense of flow when:

1) They tackle a task which they have a chance of completing.

2) They concentrate on what they are doing.

3) They have clear goals.

4) They get immediate feedback.

5) They experience a deep and effortless involvement that removes the frustrations of everyday life.

6) They enjoy a sense of control over their actions.

7) They find their concern for self disappears, but paradoxically their sense of self emerges stronger.

8) They find the experience is so enjoyable that their sense of time disappears.

"Tragedies Transformed" is the title of a study conducted by Professor Fausto Massimini of the University of Milan, who interviewed paraplegics. Many said the accident that caused paraplegia had produced both positive and negative consequences. Tragic events presented them with extremely clear goals. Learning to live again was in itself a matter of pride. People who mastered the fresh challenges experienced a clarity of purpose which they had not felt before their accidents. Lucio had been a 20-year-old gas station attendant when a motor cycle accident paralysed him below the waist. He said:

"When I became paraplegic, it was like being born again. I had to learn from scratch everything I used to know, but in a different way. I had to learn to dress myself, to use my head better. I had to become part of the environment, and use it without trying to control it . . . it took commitment, will power and patience. As far as the future is concerned, I hope to keep improving, to keep breaking through the limitations of my handicap . . . Everybody must have a purpose. After becoming a paraplegic, these improvements have become my life goal."

Franco also suffers from paraplegia. Before his accident his most intense flow experiences came from acrobatic dancing on Saturday nights, writes Mihaly. Franco, who is paralysed from the waist down, has set new targets. The most important goal in his life is to "feel that I can be of use to others, help recent victims accept their situation". Franco, Lucio and other paraplegics have focused on what they want to accomplish in their lives. Mihaly believes their example has much to teach us. He writes:

"Each of us has a picture, however vague, of what we would like to accomplish before we die. How close we get to attaining this goal becomes the measure for the quality of our lives. If it remains beyond reach, we grow resentful or resigned; if it is at least in part achieved, we experience a sense of happiness and satisfaction."

Encouragement is the first step towards helping people to find peace, but they want more than comforting words. People want the basic materials for life: food, a good home, money and satisfying work. Try tackling the following three exercises which focus on how you can help people to increase their own health, hope and happiness. Encouragement is a good start, but it isn't always enough. People must also take initiatives to shape their own futures, a fact which highlights the next theme addressed by Encouragers.

HEALTH

Three concrete things I can do to help people to increase their health

1) I can _____

2) I can _____

3) I can _____

HOPE

Three concrete things I can do to help people to increase their hope

1) I can _____

2) I can _____

3) I can _____

HAPPINESS

Three concrete things I can do to help people to increase their happiness

1) I can _____

2) I can _____

3) I can _____

Step Two:
ENTERPRISE

MAGGIE KUHN acted as an enterprising model for thousands of people around the world. During the early 1970s she and five friends reached the compulsory retirement age of 65. Disgusted at the way America devalued its older people, they created the Grey Panthers. "There's a new kind of energy that comes from late in life, a new freedom," said Maggie. She mobilised older people to claim their rights and show what they could offer society. Her initiative attracted global attention and created a worldwide membership of 70,000 Grey Panthers. Writing in *The Ageless Spirit,* she declares:

"I am having — and I say this quite candidly and gratefully — a glorious old age. Sure, I have arthritis; I have very severe arthritis in my hands. It is very hard for me to open things and turn off a light switch; there are lots of things I cannot do. I have arthritis in my knees too, and at times it's very painful and I have difficulty walking. But there's nothing wrong with my head, thank goodness, and nothing wrong with my spirit.

"Old folks need to be mentors for the young," said Maggie, "and the young need old folks just as much as we need them." She created housing co-operatives where old and young people shared accommodation. Older people offered their life-experience and wisdom; younger people offered their energy and practical skills. Maggie believed in passing on knowledge from generation to generation. Echoing the philosophy voiced by the paraplegics, she wrote:

"I believe that there has to be a purpose and a goal to life. The secret of thriving and surviving is to have a goal. Having a goal is absolutely essential, because it gives you the energy and the drive to do what you must do, and to get up when you feel like staying in bed . . . I have plenty of goals! On my 80th birthday, in fact, I vowed to myself that I would do something outrageous at least once a week, and for the past few years I've been able to live up to that promise."

YOU CAN BE
ENTERPRISING YOURSELF

Everybody is creative, everybody can be enterprising. Showing is better than telling, however, so the best way to inspire people is by being a good model yourself. The following pages offer exercises you can use to clarify your successes and resources.

MY ACHIEVEMENTS

"But I haven't achieved anything," somebody may argue. Everybody has a history of success. David, a 25-year-old social worker, tackled this exercise when suffering from low self-confidence. Drawing a line denoting the length of his life, he listed his achievements during these years. We discussed how he achieved his successes and how he could follow similar principles in his future life.

MY CREATIVE TIMES

This is more a concentrated version of the previous exercise. Think of a time in your life when you feel you have done creative work. For example: building a shed, running a course, writing a book or tackling a challenge. Describe five things you did right to make yourself creative. Conclude by planning how to follow similar paths again in the future.

MY WEALTH

"If I had more money I'd be able to follow my dreams," is a popular view. Perhaps, but enterprise calls for using resources and imagination. Create a list of all your assets: your health, life-experience, finances, relationships, talents, skills, contacts, etc. People are much wealthier than they think. Explore how you can use your assets to help you reach your goals.

YOU CAN ENCOURAGE PEOPLE TO BE ENTERPRISING

Enterprise calls for people taking responsibility. Viktor Frankl, author of *Man's Search For Meaning*, says that each of us makes a choice each moment of our lives. He writes: "Man is not free from his conditions, but he is free to take a stand towards his conditions." He speaks from terrible experience.

A prisoner in Nazi death camps, Viktor believes the people who survived often had something to live for beyond the immediate terror: they had a book to write, a relationship to share or a dream to pursue. Fortune played an enormous part, but each person faced choices each day. New arrivals found the ordeal began when the railway trucks drew into the camp sidings.

MY ACHIEVEMENTS

Make a list of all the things you feel you have achieved during your life. These can be small or big things. Start from an early age and continue until the present day. For example, here is one person's view of some things he achieved during his first 25 years.

Achievements

Age	Achievements
0	Born.
5	Survived an early illness.
	Found school difficult, so I stayed at home and invented football games.
	Asked my parents to help me learn to read.
10	Found a successful way around the system. This set the pattern for my later life.
	Encouraged both my parents during their divorce.
15	Travelled around the country by myself watching football matches. Travelled to London by myself when I was 14.
	Visited over 60 Football League grounds.
	Left school and found a job in a garage.
	Went to night school and learned how to pass exams.
	Built a good relationship with my second girlfriend.
20	Got a voluntary job working with children.
	Left the garage to do full-time voluntary work.
	Got a full-time job working with mentally-handicapped people.
	Wrote to several famous teachers asking if I could learn from them. Two offered to act as mentors. Spent a month a year learning from them.
25	Ran a halfway house for people coming out of mental hospital.

MY CREATIVE TIMES

1)   Describe a time in your life when you believe you did creative work.

●   When I _____

     _____

2)   What were you doing right then? Write five things you did right to do creative work.

●   I _____

●   I _____

●   I _____

●   I _____

●   I _____

3)   How can you follow these paths again in the future? Describe what you can do to perform creative work.

●   I can _____

●   I can _____

●   I can _____

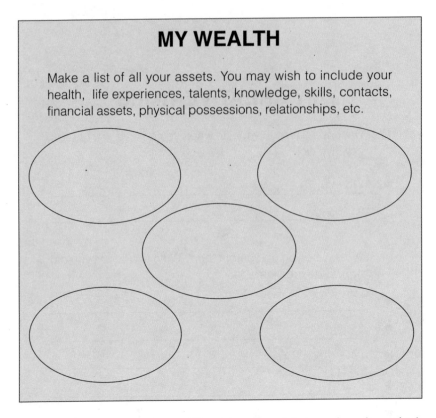

MY WEALTH

Make a list of all your assets. You may wish to include your health, life experiences, talents, knowledge, skills, contacts, financial assets, physical possessions, relationships, etc.

Recalling his own experience, Viktor describes joining a long line which shuffled towards an SS officer. The officer looked at each person and casually pointed to the left or the right.

"It was my turn," writes Viktor. "Somebody whispered to me that to be sent to the right side would mean work, the way to the left being for the sick and those incapable of work, who would be sent to a special camp. I just waited for things to take their course, the first of many such times to come. My haversack weighed me down a bit to the left, but I made an effort to walk upright. The SS man looked me over, appeared to hesitate, then put both his hands on my shoulders, I tried very hard to look smart, and he turned my shoulders very slowly until I faced right, and I moved over to that side."

Ten per cent were sent to the right and lived. Ninety per cent were sent to the left and the "showers". Viktor lived and tried to make sense of the suffering. One night he heard the cries of a prisoner caught in a nightmare. Viktor moved to wake him but drew back his hand. "At that moment," he wrote, "I became intensely conscious of the fact that no dream, no matter how horrible, could be as bad as the reality of the camp which surrounded us, and to which I was about to recall him."

Viktor survived the Nazi camps, emigrated to America and practised as a psychiatrist. Working with suicidal people, he recognised the similarity between them and prisoners in the death camps. He recalled two prisoners who talked of committing suicide. Both men used the typical argument: that they had nothing more to expect from life. The challenge was to show the men that life was still expecting something from them. Viktor continues:

"We found, in fact, that for the one it was his child whom he adored and who was waiting for him in a foreign country. For the other it was a thing, not a person. This was a scientist and he had written a series of books which still needed to be finished. His work could not be done by anyone else, any more than another person could ever take the place of the father in his child's affections . . . A man who becomes conscious of the responsibility he bears toward a human being who affectionately waits for him, or to an unfinished work, will never be able to throw away his life. He knows the 'why' for his existence, and will be able to bear almost any 'how'."

Camp life showed that people do have a choice of action, said Viktor, and prisoners who lost faith in the future were doomed. As a result of his experiences, he created Logotherapy, a form of therapy which helps people to fulfil their meaning in life.

I was 17 when John, my best friend, asked me to choose. "You are so negative," he said. "You are driving people away. You are going to be very lonely during your life." Being cynical had become a way for me to survive working in a factory. John showed I could choose between being Positive or Negative, an Encourager or a Stopper, a Creator or a Complainer. "But that is too simple," I protested. John was honest and got me to listen. He asked me to choose between being on the side of Life or Death.

YOU CAN HELP PEOPLE TO SET GOALS

Viktor Frankl, Mihaly Csikszentmihalyi and Maggie Kuhn emphasise the importance of working towards personal goals. Different people set goals on different levels. Maria, the athletics champion, clarified and followed her chosen route in life. Managers attending business courses conclude by writing action plans for improving their profits. Mothers and fathers create mental lists of the practical tasks to be completed that day. Goal setting is helpful, but it is also important to enjoy the journey.

What are your goals? Try tackling the exercise called Two Years To Live. What would be your priorities if you only had this time to live? Vivienne, a 50-year-old farmer, settled on three aims: exploring the countryside with her two grandchildren, caring for the animals, and planting trees in the fields. What would you enjoy, share or complete in the next two years? Plan how you can pursue these paths in your present life.

People may feel both happy and scared when tackling this exercise. Why? Pursuing their life-goals is like falling in love. Life is both beautiful and frightening, because this joy can suddenly be snatched away. They may also need to be patient. Focusing on priorities does not mean accomplishing everything in one day. People who pursue their A1 goal feel more at peace with themselves. They can relax, make haste slowly and enjoy the journey.

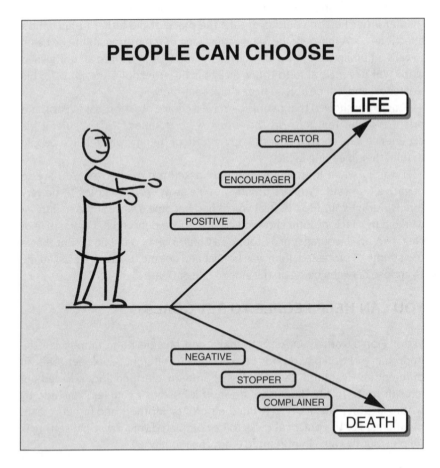

TWO YEARS TO LIVE

What would you do if you only had two years to live?
Write down all the things that you would do.

I would:

- _____
- _____
- _____
- _____
- _____

Can you do anything towards doing some of these things now
and in the next few months? Write the things you want to do.

I want:

- _____
- _____
- _____
- _____
- _____

Taking steps towards doing these things will help to ensure
that you are focusing on your A1 goals.

YOU CAN HELP PEOPLE TO BE CREATIVE

Some people seek to develop their talents by attending Creativity Workshops. Such programmes often concentrate on using three key words: "What? How? When?" They also offer a wide variety of techniques, such as Lateral Thinking, Visualisation and Whole Brain Thinking. Tools and techniques are seductive, but creativity calls for going back to basics. People must clarify their "What?" before rushing to the "How?" Let's explore how this works in practice.

Helen, a 45-year-old solicitor, attended a Creativity Workshop. Along with the other participants, she was invited to select a challenge she wanted to solve in her personal or professional life. Helen focused on helping Sally, her 15-year-old daughter, to improve her school grades. Assisted by the other workshop participants, she followed the problem-solving model shown on the next page.

Step One was to ask Helen: "What are the real results you want to achieve?" She wanted to help Sally to achieve excellent grades. Why? Helen wanted her to enter university, win a degree and gain the "passport" to job opportunities. Sally experienced problems passing exams, however, but she liked caring for animals. She already did voluntary work at the local animal rescue centre.

Forty-five minutes were spent helping Helen to clarify the real results she wanted to achieve. Looking beyond the presented problem, this turned out to be: "I want to help Sally to find work she enjoys." What might be the pluses and minuses? Pluses: Helen would offer Sally a gift for life and feel happy about doing her best as a parent. Minuses: Helen must forgo her dream of Sally attending university and also devote time to the search to find satisfying work.

Step Two was to ask Helen: "How can you do your best to achieve this result?" Along with other people on the workshop, she spent 15 minutes doing individual brainstorming. Each person was invited to write five suggestions which Helen could use to help Sally. People read out their ideas and she wrote down those she believed in. Helen added these suggestions to her own and created a list of action points. These included:

● Make a contract with Sally about whether she wants me to help her to find work she enjoys.

The three key words
for being creative:

WHAT? HOW? WHEN?

You can ask yourself:

1) WHAT IS THE REAL RESULT I WANT TO ACHIEVE?

- Focus on one goal at a time.

- Make the goal super-specific.

- Clarify the *real results* you want to achieve by reaching the goal.

- Clarify the pluses and minuses involved in reaching the goal. Decide whether you are prepared to accept the whole package.

- Complete the "What?" before moving on to the "How?"

2) HOW CAN I DO MY BEST TO ACHIEVE THIS RESULT?

- Say: "I can . . . " and brainstorm lots of ideas.

- First: Go for quantity of ideas. Second: Go for quality of ideas.

- Choose the options most likely to succeed.

3) WHEN DO I WANT TO ACHIEVE THIS RESULT?

- Make a specific action plan for achieving the goal.

- Plan how to encourage yourself on the journey.

- Start work and get some early successes.

- Spend time with her at the rescue centre. Ask her to teach me about how she cares for the animals.

- Invite her to draw a map showing all the possible places where she can work with animals. Visit these places with her at evenings and weekends.

- Talk with local vets, rescue centres and the RSPCA. Research the job prospects and qualifications required in the field.

- Encourage her to discover what qualifications she needs to find a job with animals which also pays a reasonable wage.

Step Three was to ask Helen: "When do you want to achieve these results?" She saw her daughter's 18th birthday as a crucial milestone, because Sally·must then be ready to pay her way in the world. Starting from this destination, Helen worked backwards and planned the things she must complete by each stage: two years, 18 months, 12 months, nine months, six months, three months and one month. "It's a bit like Project Management," she said, "but with feelings that are important to me and Sally." Helen wrote her short-term plan which included talking with Sally at the weekend. She could only do her best, of course, because Sally must put her heart and soul into finding satisfying work.

Creativity begins by making sure you are climbing the right mountain. Helen could have used every technique in the book to help her daughter improve at school. Intellectually stimulating perhaps, but she would be inventing elegant ways to climb the wrong mountain. Too often people confuse activity with results. Creativity starts by identifying the real "What?". Providing this is done properly, people find it relatively easy to clarify the "How?" Students can grasp these lessons early in life by learning to be creative in school.

YOU CAN ENCOURAGE ENTERPRISE IN EDUCATION

William Glasser's book *Schools Without Failure* described learning as a partnership in which students take responsibility for their own learning. Young people then form the habit of setting goals, being creative and delivering results. They are more likely to "own" the learning and integrate it into their daily lives. Responsibility is a two-way street, so the teacher must also build a good climate in the classroom. How to make this happen?

Imagine you are a teacher educating 18-year-olds in college. Welcome the students, share your goals for the year and outline the benefits to them as young people. Explain that you will do your best to make the learning attractive, but you will also need help. Describe what you see as: a) Your responsibilities as a teacher and, b) Their responsibilities as students. Contracting is vital, so make an agreement about working together for the academic year.

Invite the students to form small groups. Ask each group to create a poster like that shown on the next page. They are then to present their ideas to the class. (Students will obviously have their own views about the responsibilities.) Discuss the students' suggestions and add your views. Invite two volunteers to condense the ideas, create a final poster and present it back to the class. Finalise the contract with the students and display the poster in the classroom. Make sure both you and the students keep to the contract.

People of all ages respond well to this exercise. Contracting is a key skill which creates the foundation for living and working together in families, schools, teams, businesses and nations. Encouragers make agreements with students about the "rules" for doing good work and fulfil their part of the bargain, which includes helping the students to develop their talents.

YOU CAN HELP STUDENTS TO BE CREATIVE

Everybody is creative. Maybe this view sounds too romantic, but Howard Gardner's work on the Seven Intelligences has changed the educational agenda. His book *Frames Of Mind* describes how every person has different ways of learning, and favours using different kinds of intelligence. These include:

- Verbal intelligence.
- Logical intelligence.
- Musical intelligence.
- Visual intelligence.
- Physical intelligence.
- Interpersonal intelligence.
- Intrapersonal intelligence.
  (An understanding of values, emotions and life-patterns.)

CONTRACT

THE TEACHER'S RESPONSIBILITY IS:	THE STUDENTS' RESPONSIBILITY IS:
● To be a good model for the students.	● To prepare properly for the lessons.
● To be on time for lessons.	● To be on time for lessons.
● To be positive and enthusiastic.	● To be positive and enthusiastic.
● To make clear learning contracts with students and, whenever possible, with parents.	● To make clear learning contracts with the teacher and, whenever possible, with parents.
● To describe the goals which apply to each lesson.	● To be clear on what they want to achieve from the lesson.
● To make lessons enjoyable and effective.	● To work hard and do their best in the lessons.
● To make complicated things simple.	● To encourage and help each other.
● To show how students can use the learning in their daily lives.	● To think how they can use the learning in their daily lives.
● To be fair and honest.	● To be fair and honest.
● To encourage the students.	● To encourage the teacher.
● To be creative and also expect students to be responsible and do their best.	● To be creative and give something back to the school and to the community.

Thomas Armstrong has built on Howard Gardner's work and written a superb book for parents whose children are experiencing difficulties in school. Called *In Their Own Way*, it provides a treasure chest of ideas for encouraging children. He begins his book by saying:

"Six years ago I quit my job as a learning disabilities specialist. I had to. I no longer believed in learning disabilities . . . It was then that I turned to the concept of learning differences as an alternative to learning disabilities. I realised that the millions of children being referred to as learning-disabled weren't handicapped, but instead had unique learning styles that the schools did not understand."

"Everyone has all seven kinds of intelligence in different proportions. Your child may be a great reader but a poor maths student, a wonderful drawer but clumsy out on the playing field. Children can even show a wide range of strengths and weaknesses within one area of intelligence. Your child may write very well but have difficulty with spelling or handwriting, read poorly but be a superb story-teller, play an excellent game of basketball but stumble on the dance floor."

With apologies to Howard Gardner, I have changed and merged some of his terms. So it would be useful for readers to catch up with his latest thinking. But in every classroom you will find children who learn in different ways. These include:

The Verbal Child

> They learn through listening and talking. They are sensitive to sounds and the meanings of words. They may eventually choose to work as, for example, a journalist or writer.

The Logical Child

> They learn through reasoning and identifying logical or numerical patterns. They may eventually choose to work as, for example, a scientist or a mathematician.

The Musical Child

> They learn through producing and appreciating musical rhythms. They may eventually choose to work as, for example, a composer or musician.

The Visual Child

> They learn through seeing and perceiving what Gardner calls "the visual-spatial world". They do this accurately and may eventually choose to work as, for example, a sculptor or navigator.

The Physical Child

> They learn through moving their body and handling objects skilfully. They may eventually choose to work as, for example, an athlete or a dancer.

The Social Child

They learn through interaction and watching how people play, live and work together. They may eventually choose to work in, for example, the caring professions or service business.

The Individual Child

They learn through making sense of their experience and identifying patterns in life. Preferring to learn alone, later in life they will face the challenge of making a living. They will need to become both soul-wise and street-wise. They may eventually become, for example, an artist, educator or somebody else who passes on their knowledge about life.

THE CREATIVE CHILD

THE VERBAL CHILD

THE INDIVIDUAL CHILD

THE LOGICAL CHILD

THE SOCIAL CHILD

THE MUSICAL CHILD

THE PHYSICAL CHILD

THE VISUAL CHILD

The Key School in Indianapolis applies the ideas of Howard Gardner and Mihaly Csikszentmihalyi. Located in the inner city, it is four times over-subscribed, so students are chosen by lottery. Key's eight founding teachers believe that all 160 children bring natural strengths to the school. Each child is also able to develop all seven intelligences. While covering the conventional Three Rs, the teachers use different methods to nurture the children's talents. Marie Winn, writing in *The Good Health Magazine*, describes her visit to the Key School.

"In Room 25 one day last winter, 22 highly concentrated little violinists are eagerly honing their musical intelligence to the tune of (or somewhere vaguely near it) "Frosty the Snowman" . . . In Room 17 Carol Forbes is demonstrating the difference between a small triangle and a large circle — in Spanish — a lesson that combines exercises in both linguistic and spatial intelligence . . . Intelligences run amok in Room 10, where a two-month-long schoolwide effort has produced a spectacular re-creation of a tropical rain forest.'

"It is hard to remember that this is not a special school for gifted children, but one whose racially and ethnically diverse population is chosen by lottery, with more than a third of the students qualifying for free or reduced-price school lunch . . . In its third year of operation, the Key School shows every sign of being a runaway success. Scores on the standardised tests show that the two intelligences most valued in our education system are thriving. Only five children in the entire school failed to reach the acceptable level mandated by the school district."

Encouragers work to make school the most hopeful place in our society. Teachers can help students to learn the basic educational skills, develop their natural talents and find or create work they love. Many of us recall golden moments when our teacher said: "You are special. You are creative. You can follow your dream in life." Encouragement only takes a minute, but the memory lasts for ever. School can equip young people to take charge of their lives and create satisfying work.

YOU CAN ENCOURAGE ENTERPRISE IN WORK

Antonio Paz Martinez has inspired many people to take initiatives. After the 1985 earthquake wrecked the poor neighbourhoods of central Mexico City, he set up an organisation for homeless people living in tents. This was called

Campamentos Unidos (Tent-Dwellers United). His initial focus was to help people to build new homes, but this has evolved into them shaping their future lives. An Ashoka Fellow, Antonio explains:

"People in the community choose their own houses. The drawings were also done by an architect that also lives in our colonia. It's important that people could see the prototype of the houses and play with the furniture inside it, getting a feeling for the space available."

House verandas overlook the traditional courtyard which nurtures a sense of community. Women sew, cook food and take other jobs to supplement the family income. Living close together, it is natural to combine their talents and organise co-operatives. Antonio teaches them the business and legal skills needed to succeed in the market. The 1988 Ashoka report continues:

"Noting that the public supply of tortilla in central Mexico city runs out by 2.00 in the afternoon, mothers organised in one of Antonio's groups are producing the missing supply. Others raise chickens on the rooftops. Another organisation he's building, that distributes basic consumer goods (e.g. coffee and powdered milk) at prices even below the government's, provides the organisation's own retail distribution arm for such products.

"A number of other products grew out of Campamentos Unidos's initial concentration on helping the tent-dwellers build new homes. A growing carpentry group makes furniture inexpensively from building demolition wastes. It plans to begin moving down its distribution chain soon by opening its own warehouse."

Antonio is idealistic and street-wise. Staying ahead of the market calls for intelligent analysis, so he has created an education centre for the network of small producers. The Centre contains six departments: legal, education and training, research, ecology and environment, co-operative organisation and communication. Antonio is empowering people to shape their own futures.

YOU CAN HELP INDIVIDUALS TO BE ENTERPRISING

Paul Hawken reached millions of budding entrepreneurs through his American public television series *Growing a Business*. He speaks with authority, having built several successful businesses, starting with one of the first natural food stores in the USA. Based in Boston, the Erewhon Trading Company was grossing $25,000 a day in 1973. He later co-founded the mail order firm Smith & Hawken. Located in Mill Valley, California, the company has built a reputation for delivering high quality tools around the world. Paul believes strongly in small businesses, which play a key role in most nations' economies, and provides advice for people aiming to start their own firms.

BUILD ON YOUR STRENGTHS

Paul advises people to develop their talents and produce quality. Even in a recession, customers will pay for quality products delivered in a quality way. What do you do best? Try tackling the exercise called My Strengths. Brainstorm ten things you do well, big or small things, then describe your top three talents. Quality will always find a market, we are told, so how can you create a successful business?

MY STRENGTHS

Brainstorm the things you do well, these can be big or small things, then list your top three qualities. Follow this by brainstorming and then clarifying ways you can earn money doing some of these things.

My strengths are:

1) _____

2) _____

3) _____

How I can earn money doing some of these things:

1) _____

2) _____

3) _____

RECREATE SOMETHING THAT HAS BEEN LOST

People are attracted to nostalgia: so recreate something which they believe has been lost for ever. The friendly small town bank; the reliable mail-order firm; the honest garage; the quality ice-cream shop; the traditional cheese store; the aromatic coffee shop; the company that fixes mistakes without complaint. Be honest, deliver quality and make people feel special.

"Remember that in business you are never trying to 'beat' the competition," writes Paul. "You are trying to give your customer something other than what they are receiving from the competition. It is a waste of time and energy trying to beat the competition because the customer doesn't care about that rivalry."

TOO MUCH MONEY IS WORSE THAN TOO LITTLE

Businesses suffer from a lack of imagination, not capital, says Paul. Too much money tends to replace creativity. Companies without money are hungry; they must dream, imagine and improvise. Companies awash with money try to buy solutions. They lavish vast amounts on consultants, lawyers, clever accountants, publicity agents and marketing studies. Cash and creativity are both necessary, but make sure you balance them properly.

ENTREPRENEURS ARE RISK-AVOIDERS

"The common wisdom holds that entrepreneurs love to take risks," says Paul. "That's mostly hype." Entrepreneurs are like mountain climbers. They set clear goals, clarify their strategy and anticipate ways to tackle problems. Onlookers think the mountaineer is gambling, but the climber would risk more by not following his or her dream. "Once the entrepreneur has seen how to create a product or service to meet demand," says Paul, "much of what the outsider perceives as risk in the situation is erased." On the other hand, he adds, risk-avoiders do not always make good entrepreneurs.

BUSINESS TESTS CHARACTER

Business teaches you a lot about yourself, says Paul: "The moment you enter the world of business — as a provider, not merely as a consumer — you will have a hundred opportunities a day to act beneficially or wrongly, to deal with people fairly or otherwise, to enhance your social environment or pollute it." You will face split-second decisions: to be honest or to lie; to deliver quality or to cut corners; to care for your customers or to give shoddy service. Business continually tests character.

BUSINESS WILL ALWAYS HAVE PROBLEMS

Paul once searched for magic solutions. Providing he read more books by business gurus, he felt, one day he would find business nirvana.

Enlightenment would make all his problems disappear. The truth hit him one sunny autumn afternoon:

"I had my nirvana, all right, but it was the opposite of what I had been seeking. On that pretty afternoon the actual truth finally struck me: I would always have problems. In fact, problems signify that the business is in a rapid learning phase. The revelation was liberating. I couldn't understand why other people hadn't told me this earlier."

Problems create either energy or paralysis, says Paul. Good managers make problems interesting and mobilise people's energies to find solutions. Bad managers present problems as threats, criticisms or things to be ignored. They issue memos, blame others or say it is the customer's fault. Get used to problems, says Paul, they are an eternal part of everyday business life.

DEVELOP TRADESKILLS

"Tradeskill is what you learn as a kid while running the paper route, working in your uncle's store, or starting an over-the-counter market in baseball cards," says Paul. "Tradeskills are demonstrated in abundance in the open-air wholesale produce and fish markets in New York and Hong Kong and every other big city. They are evident at horse and cattle auctions."

Tradeskills spell the difference between success and failure in a business. People who have them demonstrate the following characteristics:

- They know how to handle money, how to buy and how to pay.
- They feel comfortable haggling in the street market where the prices are negotiable.
- They feel comfortable with strangers.
- They understand what people want, how much they will pay and how they make their decision.
- They know how to read the signals of the market place.
- They know how to approach a given product or market niche.
- They have a sixth sense that enables them to make quick decisions, rather than get bogged down in months of meetings, brainstorming and market studies.

"Most of us know whether we possess tradeskill," says Paul, "If you haven't got it, the best thing to do is to recognise this and plan your life and career accordingly." You can still build a business, but complement your strengths with people who have tradeskills. Success then depends on harnessing the talents of the team. How to make this happen?

YOU CAN HELP TEAMS TO BE ENTERPRISING

"Five of my team already take initiatives every day; the problem is they do their own thing," says Derek, Director of the White House community for teenagers. "Two of my team sit passively waiting for instructions, then they complain. How can I manage this mixture?"

What would you advise Derek to do? How can he co-ordinate the seven youth workers to build an enterprising team? One way to start is by returning to the agreed goals for the White House: "We want to encourage the young people, our colleagues and our sponsors." Derek can meet each person to agree on their contribution to achieving these targets. The next step is to make clear contracts about other aspects of their behaviour.

Clear contracting is a key factor in personal and professional relationships. Clarity gives people the freedom to be creative because they like to know where they stand. They like to know the team's goals, their personal goals and the freedom they have to achieve these goals. People also like to know the "rules" for working together in a team. Which behaviours are acceptable? Which behaviours are unacceptable? Good leaders strike the right balance between structure and spontaneity. While ensuring that people follow the agreed guidelines, they give everybody the chance to use their individual talents.

Derek can channel the team's energies by tackling the exercise called My Contracts With My Team. He can write down the agreements he wants to make with all the staff at the White House. His final list might read something like this:

TEAM CONTRACTS

I want to make the following contracts with my team. I want us:

● To start meetings on time.
● To start by sharing successes from the previous week.

- To speak one at a time during the meeting.
- To be honest and give each other clear messages, rather than talk in the corridor.
- To stick to one subject at a time and, wherever possible, reach an agreed conclusion.
- To go beyond criticising other people and instead give positive suggestions.
- To encourage people to dare to try different approaches, providing these contribute to achieving the overall goals at the White House.

MY CONTRACTS WITH MY TEAM

Make a list of the contracts you would like to make with everybody in your team. These can cover any aspect of your work together.

THE CONTRACTS I WANT TO MAKE WITH MY TEAM

- _____
  _____
- _____
  _____
- _____
  _____
- _____
  _____
- _____
  _____

Clear contracting forms the basis for creating good habits, but such agreements will only work if people enter them voluntarily. How does this work in practice? Derek can simply say to his team: "I would like to make some contracts with you." People buy pluses, they won't buy minuses, so he must give reasons for making the contracts and describe the benefits. He can also introduce one topic at a time, rather than issue a long shopping list. An alternative approach can be used if he wants to give team members a greater sense of ownership. Staff can be invited to brainstorm and then agree on the contracts they want to make with each other about their work at the White House.

Derek can move on to co-ordinating the activities of the individual staff by tackling the exercise called My Contracts With Individual People. First: He can write the names of people with whom he wants to make contracts. Second: He can list the specific contracts he wants to make with each of these people. Derek's final list may look something like the one shown below.

INDIVIDUAL CONTRACTS

I want to make the following contracts with individual people in my team.

DAWN

- That she continues to develop her talents as an art therapist and do outstanding work with the teenagers. We can make contracts about how I can support her in this work.

- That she passes on her knowledge about art therapy to another member of staff, rather than keep it to herself. How? She can invite Dave to join some classes. He wants to use some of the ideas in the school lessons he runs for the teenagers.

- That she keeps other staff informed about what she is doing in her classes. Sometimes she makes decisions, such as sending the teenagers into town to do art projects, without informing other people. She could create more goodwill by telling other staff about forthcoming activities.

CLIFF

- That he decides whether or not he wants to work at the White House.

- That, if he does, he gets to work on time, dresses in clean clothes and washes his hair more regularly.

- That, if he decides to move on, to leave in a way that is good for both him and people at the White House. We can agree on how this can be achieved.

MY CONTRACTS WITH INDIVIDUAL PEOPLE

Make a list of the people who you want to make contracts with in your team. Then list what you want to make contracts about with each of these people.

THE PERSON

- _____

**THE CONTRACTS I WANT
TO MAKE WITH THIS PERSON**

- _____
- _____
- _____

THE PERSON

- _____

**THE CONTRACTS I WANT
TO MAKE WITH THIS PERSON**

- _____
- _____
- _____

Derek can hold contracting meetings with each youth worker at the White House. Most interviews will be pleasant, but he must be also prepared for somebody to turn the tables by saying: "I want to make some contracts with you, Derek." Tougher interviews will call for being honest, bringing issues to the surface and finding solutions. Derek will be tackling a challenge which confronts many leaders today: he must co-ordinate the talents and activities of individual knowledge workers. Why are such people so difficult to manage?

MANAGING KNOWLEDGE WORKERS

"Enterprise isn't a problem in our company, but how do you get creative people to work in teams?" asked the chief executive of an advertising agency. "Our staff are our greatest asset because their know-how is the company. They go home every night and we hope they will return in the morning. We then face another difficulty. How do you get individual knowledge workers to work towards the company's goals?"

Modern organisations depend on the know-how of their staff. Schools, hospitals, computer companies, banks and law firms must retain vital knowledge workers. Staff who leave take with them their expertise, contacts and future products. Employers spend time and money recouping the losses. Some are tackling this challenge by asking: "How can we attract talented people? How can we maintain their loyalty? How can we get them to work well together in teams?" Although the research is still in its infancy, it's important to recognise what motivates knowledge workers.

1)   They are individuals

Knowledge workers tend to be individuals who experience frustration in large groups. They emphasise "personal chemistry", however, and enjoy working with like-minded people on projects. Knowledge workers want the best "tools for their trade". They will pay extra for an Apple Macintosh which is user-friendly, for example, rather than buy a computer which suppresses their personality. Speaking their minds brings benefits and problems to an organisation, they bring freshness but can also be blunt. Managers must develop strategies for handling the interface between difficult knowledge workers and other people in the team.

2) They have integrity

They have strong personal and professional values. Knowledge workers prefer to work for organisations that translate their values into real action, rather than those that pay lip service to mission statements. Professional integrity is also vital. They believe in being true to their science, art or craft and seldom compromise. They place a high value on quality of life and quality of work.

3) They are inner-directed

Knowledge workers formulate their opinions by exploring their own values, thoughts and feelings. Previous generations were frequently outer-directed, looking for guidance from authorities, such as the Church, politicians and other experts. Writing in *Millennium: Towards Tomorrow's Society*, Francis Kinsman points out that inner-directed people are gaining more professional and economic influence. This is changing the agenda in our society. Knowledge workers are choosing to live in the countryside, send their children to small village schools and concentrate on their own professional development. Status is nice, but it takes second place to quality of life.

4) They are intelligent

Knowledge workers have read more books, visited more countries and studied more "best practice" than any previous generation. Many are extremely bright, but seldom feel stretched intellectually. The senior team of a computer company I worked with recently were experts in their own profession, but were hungry to grasp fresh ideas from other fields, such as theories of global change. Knowledge workers want to "know". Knowledge is their currency and provides the passport to professional development.

5) They are innovative

They prefer to find solutions, rather than endlessly to discuss problems. Knowledge workers get upset in meetings when other staff argue about seemingly irrelevant details or revisit old battlefields. They feel irritated with politicians, union leaders and managers who talk in "old speak" or rehash redundant arguments unsuitable for the 21st century. Knowledge workers prefer to ask: "What are the results we want to achieve? How can we do our best to achieve them?" They enjoy thinking outside the accepted parameters to find solutions. Innovation makes them feel alive and provides the energy to grow.

Businesses face great challenges motivating such individuals to increase profits. Knowledge workers feel passionately about their jobs. They take a pride in their products and want to develop as professionals. Few are turned on by the thought of stockpiling cash for shareholders. Money is seen as a means, to improve the quality of life for themselves and their loved ones, rather than as an end. While wanting *enough* money, they fail to see any sense in breaking their backs continually to improve profits. Businesses that find ways to inspire knowledge workers will reap a rich harvest.

Managing talented people is a full-time role. It is definitely not a secondary job to be tackled in a few odd moments. Knowledge workers must also fulfil their part of the bargain, however, by committing themselves to reaching the team's goals. Clear contracting plays a vital part in co-ordinating their desire to be enterprising and to develop their gifts. Creative people respond best when they build on their strengths, set clear goals, work with people they respect, receive ongoing encouragement, develop their skills and produce results. They will then work hard to build a successful team.

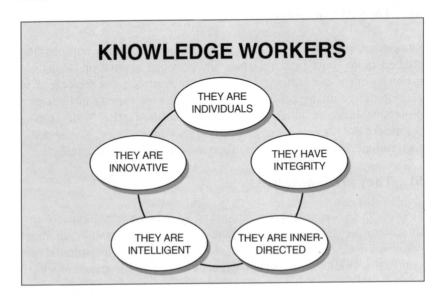

YOU CAN HELP ORGANISATIONS TO BE ENTERPRISING

"Sports Hotels wants its people to take initiatives and do their best," said Lynn, the managing director, "so we aim to build a coaching culture." The company follows the Coaching Model (see next page), which is more fluid than it looks. Sometimes the Coaches and Co-ordinators must also become the Creators. Running this type of company calls for a radical change in roles. How does this work in practice?

Senior managers are the Coaches and remain answerable to the shareholders. They must create the strategy, gain commitment from their people and guide the company to success. They must also recognise their strengths and limits. Lynn can sell business on an "executive to executive" level, for example, but she cannot compose restaurant menus, sell advertisements and lead windsurfing lessons on the lake. She relies on managers and staff to serve the customers and collect the cash. Sports Hotels' senior team must give these people the support they need to do the job.

Senior managers have years of wisdom to share with people embarking on their careers. How can they pass on their knowledge? They can act as good models, work alongside front-line staff and give them encouragement. Experienced managers can develop their coaching skills. When watching a staff member, they can ask themselves: "First: What is the person doing well? How can I help him to build on these strengths? Second: What can he do even better and how? How can I communicate this message in a way he can accept?" Older managers can then pass on their wisdom to young people who have the energy and passion to build the business.

Middle managers are the Co-ordinators who translate the strategy into action. They say to the front-line staff: "We want to provide superb service to customers. We also want to make profits. What help do you need from us to make this happen?" The hotel receptionists may reply: "Start by installing a new telephone system." Managers must then step back to clarify what they can and cannot provide in the present financial year. Everybody is happy if the answer is: "Yes, you can have a new switchboard." Budget constraints may intervene, however, producing a "No". Managers and receptionists must then pool their creativity and keep working until they find a satisfactory solution. Co-ordinators serve the people who serve the customers.

Front-line staff are the Creators who create wealth, customer satisfaction and future business. Sports Hotels' front-liners include:

- Receptionists, cleaning staff and restaurant staff. People who answer telephones, meet customers, take orders and

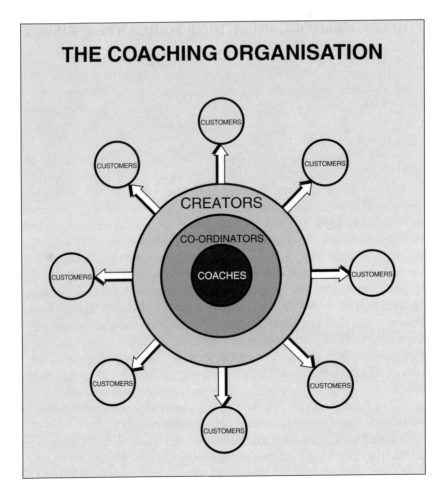

THE COACHING ORGANISATION

cook meals. They aim to give friendly, efficient and individual service to customers.

● Activity leaders. People who lead events such as aerobics, windsurfing and rock climbing. They also build long-term relationships with customers.

● Sales staff. People who consult with the Activity Leaders to develop new services and products. They market and sell these activities to individuals, organisations and companies.

"Practise what you preach", is good advice to leaders: Lynn's colleagues took these words to heart. Before announcing their desire to build a coaching culture, they spent two days attending a Coaching Programme, followed by three months applying the ideas at senior level. Why? First: They wanted to understand what coaching meant in practice. Second: They wanted to explore the pluses and minuses involved in coaching and decide whether or not to adopt this approach. Third: They wanted to practise the coaching skills and produce successful results before going public. A red thread ran through all the exercises which they tackled on the Coaching Programme, three of which are described on the following pages. Coaching means encouraging people to do their best.

1)   The Good Coach

Write the name of somebody you believe to be a good coach. This can be somebody in business, sport, the arts or any walk of life. Write five things that you believe they did well. Describe how you can follow these paths in your own way to encourage people to do their best.

2)   The Coaching Organisation

Bearing in mind what good coaches do right, describe what you believe your organisation can do to encourage people to do their best. For example: Promote good people-managers, introduce a profit share, sack all negative managers, etc.

3)   Coaching: My Action Plan

Write the names of all the people in your team. Describe each person's strengths and areas for improvement. Write the specific things you can do to encourage them to do their best. Share your action plan with your team. Report on what you have done at the next monthly meeting.

Sports Hotels adopted the coaching model to inspire their people to be enterprising. Other companies prefer to introduce more formal methods for tapping their staff's know-how. Sometimes they call in outside experts, such as the Swedish company described in the next section.

The ForeSight Group educate people to become entrepreneurs within companies. Such innovators are sometimes called "intrapreneurs". Based in Sigtuna, the group was founded by Lennart Boksjo, Sven G. Atterhead and Gustaf Delin. During the past 12 years they have fostered entrepreneurship in

THE GOOD COACH

1) Write the name of somebody who you believe coached and encouraged people to do their best. This can be a person in business, sport, the arts or any walk of life.

   • _____

2) What did they do right to encourage people to do their best? Write five things that you believe they did well to be a good coach. Be as specific as possible.

   • _____

   • _____

   • _____

   • _____

   • _____

3) How can you follow these paths in your own way to encourage people to do their best? Be as specific as possible.

   • _____

   • _____

   • _____

THE COACHING ORGANISATION

Bearing in mind what good coaches do right, describe what you believe your organisation can do to encourage people to do their best. For example: promote good people-managers, introduce a profit share, sack all negative managers, etc. Be as specific as possible.

● _____

_____

_____

● _____

_____

_____

● _____

_____

_____

● _____

_____

_____

● _____

_____

COACHING: MY ACTION PLAN

Write the names of all the people in your team. Describe their strengths, their areas for improvement and the specific things you can do to encourage them to do their best.

The person's name

● _____

Their strengths: what they do well

● _____

● _____

● _____

**Their areas for improvement:
What they can do better and how**

● _____

● _____

How I can encourage them to do their best

● I can _____

● I can _____

● I can _____

businesses across the world. Art Fry, who invented Post-It notes at 3M, showed it was possible to be creative inside a company, but such people are the exception, say ForeSight. Innovators often spend 80 per cent of their energy fighting the corporate culture and only have 20 per cent left to pursue their idea to its conclusion.

Writing in *Second To None*, Charles Garfield describes how Sven, Lennart and Gustaf take budding entrepreneurs through five steps on the road towards getting their first customer.

Step One: They get senior management commitment

ForeSight meet the senior managers to outline their approach. Companies thrive on the passion and professionalism of their people, they argue, and it is possible to harness this energy. They can help the company:

- To nurture and co-ordinate their people's desire to be enterprising.

- To identify entrepreneurs within the company and help them to implement their ideas.

- To work systematically with these internal entrepreneurs in an intensive action learning programme.

- To help to build an entrepreneurial climate in the company.

Senior managers must see how the programme will help the company to reach its goals. Commitment from the top plays a key part in helping the programme to succeed.

Step Two: They share the entrepreneurship techniques with the senior managers

ForeSight invite senior managers to tackle the company's strategic issues by thinking and acting like entrepreneurs. Outside speakers from innovative companies and fields such as sports psychology and theatre present fresh thinking to widen their horizons. Sven, Lennart and Gustaf also introduce imaginative techniques required to bring an idea to market. Senior managers then apply these entrepreneurial skills to real-life challenges facing the business.

Step Three: They encourage the entrepreneurs to emerge through self-selection

"Entrepreneurs have three things in common," says Lennart. "They are self-selecting. They have a vision. They make it happen." ForeSight practises this philosophy by inviting company employees to attend an information meeting about entrepreneurship. The chief executive starts by explaining why the company needs people to implement new ideas. ForeSight then gives an overview of the programme. Companies with 1,500 employees can normally expect between seventy to eighty people to attend the meeting.

Step Four: They invite interested people to an interview

This is a mutual interview. People get the chance to ask more detailed questions, while ForeSight discovers more about their ability to be entrepreneurs. For example: Individuals are asked to describe three situations where they worked successfully and three situations which they found frustrating. One hundred questions later they are invited to reflect on the joy and pain of becoming an entrepreneur and, if they are still interested, to apply for a place on the programme.

Step Five: They educate the entrepreneurs

ForeSight coaches people for a year. The programme includes studying good models, thinking creatively, contacting customers and producing commercial results. People meet every six to eight weeks and have three goals:

- To work on their own projects.

- To develop a business plan.

- To get their first customer.

Budding entrepreneurs are forced to work with limited resources. Why? "People are working in companies with large resources, but their own resources are deliberately limited, so that they have to use their brains. A small company often captures market share from a larger company. Why? They do it with their brains, not their brawn." ForeSight fosters what it calls "creative frugality".

Prophets have little honour in their own country, we are told, and people often find it hard to sell a creative idea in their own workplace. Try tackling the exercise called My Entrepreneurial Idea. Think of a new service, product or other project you want to pursue in your own work. What will be the benefits to you, the organisation and the customer? How can you get a sponsor? How can you market the idea? How can you get your first customer? Describe how you can translate your dream into reality.

"We have found that there are innovative people everywhere," say ForeSight. "Provide the right climate, and people implement good ideas which result in profits. Such entrepreneurs then become role models for other employees. The whole company becomes more exciting and open to innovation." Sven, Lennart and Gustaf continue to run programmes for companies all over the world.

MY ENTREPRENEURIAL IDEA

THE IDEA IS:

- _____

_____

THE BENEFITS WILL BE:

FOR MYSELF	FOR THE CUSTOMERS	FOR THE ORGANISATION
● _____	● _____	● _____
● _____	● _____	● _____
● _____	● _____	● _____

THE PLAN FOR GETTING THE FIRST CUSTOMER IS:

- _____
- _____
- _____

YOU CAN ENCOURAGE ENTERPRISE ACROSS THE PLANET

Nicholas Albery is both a visionary and an implementer. He is caring, creative and, in the best possible way, just a little bit crazy. The Albery family has run theatres in London's West End for years, and Nicholas says much of his education took place backstage. Inspired by Robert Jungk's work in Austria, in 1985 he founded the Institute for Social Inventions. He defines a social invention as a new and imaginative way of tackling a social problem or improving the quality of life. Writing the Foreword to *The Book Of Visions: An Encyclopedia of Social Innovations*, Anita Roddick explains:

"That is why I am so fond of the Institute for Social Inventions. We all have visions of a better world. Far too often we treat them as mere dreams, precisely because they are not linked to tasks. The Institute gives voice to the many incremental but bold tasks people have invented to take us towards our visions — to make hope in this world."

Nicholas runs workshops throughout Europe, and similar centres have been set up in Sweden, Russia and Germany. The UK Institute now runs an annual competition to publicise social inventions, with cash prizes for the winners. Here are three ideas.

The Catalogue of Hope

Robert Jungk founded The International Futures Library in Salzburg, which has collected over 600 social inventions from around the world. *The Catalogue of Hope* describes many of these ideas and it is planned to publish a similar book every two years. The know-how is also preserved in a Data Bank of Hope. People can tap into the bank to get information about social inventions for building a better world.

Wildlife areas around hospitals

Pat Hartridge says her idea was born in November 1984. She spent two grey weeks in the isolation unit of the Churchill Hospital in Oxford, awaiting diagnosis of Legionnaires' Disease. Her hospital stay was enlivened by a robin which perched on a wall outside her window. A string of nuts would produce a bluetit or two, she thought, and a birdtable would be better than TV. Wildlife areas could spring up around hospitals. Birds, bees and butterflies would be attracted closer to the wards and be seen by the patients. Pat described her ideas to local nurses and suggested ways to create the wildlife areas. The aims would be:

- To bring life, joy and colour closer to the ward.

- To create an interest outside the daily routine of the ward and to encourage visitors to bring gifts of bird seed rather than flowers.

- To encourage patients who are keen to record sightings of various species to add this information to the local nature conservancy records.

- To invite visiting speakers to talk about wildlife topics. They would increase knowledge and add enjoyment to the observation.

- To enlist the help of volunteers from nearby schools to care for the maintenance of the sites once they were established.

The Churchill Hospital was particularly enthusiastic and, with active help from the Assistant Nursing Officer, Mrs Patterson, it planned for the areas to be planted. Pat continues:

"My original idea — for two or three gardens to be planted and maintained by volunteers from the hospital and local schools — was defeated by its own success. The site proved so rich in likely sites that a more organised workforce was obviously required and I got the Berks, Bucks and Oxon Naturalists' Trust to act as agents for me through their MSC Community Programme . . . The Royal Society for Nature Conservation has since put together a research report and project pack on how to get such hospital wildlife gardens off the ground . . . There are now a large number of hospital wildlife gardens in progress or under consideration in the UK."

Adopt-a-Planet

The "Adopt-a-Planet" Competition is sponsored by the Gulbenkian Foundation. Any school class or youth club can enter the competition, which focuses on anti-vandalism and anti-graffiti projects. They "adopt" a local vandalised area and improve this part of the neighbourhood. Young people submit "before" and "after" photographs to the Foundation, which gives the overall winner a prize of £1,000.

George Farmer School in Holbeach, Lincolnshire, won the top prize in 1991. One class adopted a disused pond in Holbeach, which they felt had become "an eyesore, a dumping site and a general embarrassment". Pupils persuaded a local contractor to excavate the pond. They then cleared the area and planted shrubs, trees and wild flower seeds. Police and local farmers kept watch over the area to prevent future dumping. Pupils spent the prize money on a bird table, nesting boxes, benches and another small pond. Adopt-a-Planet encourages young people to act local and think global.

How can you encourage people across the planet? One way is to empower people to take charge of their own health, hope and happiness.

YOU CAN HELP PEOPLE TO TAKE CHARGE OF THEIR OWN HEALTH

Staying alive is the most basic human right. Tribal peoples have pursued their own ways of life for centuries, but many are now threatened by speculators and more dominant cultures. Survival International was set up in 1969 to assist the 200 million tribal people around the world. It aims:

- To help tribal peoples to exercise their right to survival and self-determination.

- To ensure that the interests of tribal peoples are properly presented in all decisions affecting their future.

- To secure for tribal peoples the ownership and use of adequate land and other resources and seek recognition of their rights over traditional land.

Humanity must encourage diversity if we are to survive. Survival therefore addresses three issues. First: It asserts the rights of tribal peoples to their own ways of life. Second: It shows us that nurturing diversity is in our own self-interest. Third: It works for the recognition of human values over economic and political expediency. Stephen Corry, the Director General, writes in *Replenishing the Earth*:

"Tribal peoples are well able to articulate their own defence if given the chance. And, of course, they do this better than any intermediary can. What we can provide more easily than they can is the knowledge of the outside, comparisons with other countries, analyses of international laws and forums and a general bringing together of widespread concern into a sharp focus — in brief, an efficient international organisation with thousands behind it.

"A few years ago the Guayami Indians of Panama were threatened by the copper mine project of a UK based multi-national. We put the Indians in touch with Australian Aboriginals who had suffered at the hands of the same mining giant. They were able to explain how the company's promises of prosperity masked inevitable devastation. The Indians and Survival campaigned vigorously against it, and happily the mine was not built."

Survival focuses specifically on the tribal people's right to their land. Why? Land provides all their food, medicines, building materials and spiritual meaning. Put a mine on an Australian sacred site and you put a knife straight into the heart of an Aboriginal people's heritage, says Stephen. You cut off roots which nourish their souls and which may be 40,000 or 50,000 years old. Tribal peoples may or may not have concepts of ownership; they may not have paper titles; but the land is theirs, by moral right and by law. The 30-year-old international law on tribal populations states that they have full legal right to their land. Governments which flout this law are acting illegally.

Tribal peoples have much to offer us, says Stephen; they have already given us food and medicines. Many belong to viable societies with a sense of purpose and community which some modern nations might envy. Tribal peoples will survive against extraordinary odds, but they need support from concerned people throughout the world. Survival International forges alliances with the tribal peoples and helps them to shape their own futures. It focuses on the most basic human right: the right to life.

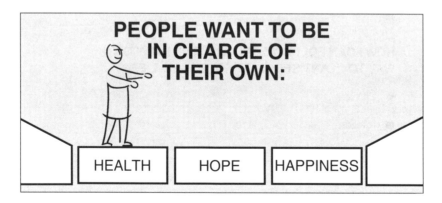

PEOPLE WANT TO BE IN CHARGE OF THEIR OWN:

HEALTH   HOPE   HAPPINESS

YOU CAN HELP PEOPLE TO TAKE CHARGE OF THEIR OWN HOPE

"How can one person spread hope across the planet?" a person may ask. The seeds planted in one place often spread to other nations. Writing in *The Healing Power of Doing Good*, Allan Luks explains the value of looking beyond the immediate results.

"Norman Cousins, who spent some time with Albert Schweitzer in Africa, pointed out to me that Schweitzer's small hospital was never able to improve the health of people around it significantly, but it did spur the development of many other hospitals in poor countries. So, in the end there

---

PEOPLE WHOSE WORK IS STILL·ALIVE

Write a list of people who have died but whose work still gives people hope. For example: I believe the work of Abraham Maslow, Alexander Calder and Virginia Satir will continue to encourage present and future generations. Describe how you can follow their paths in your own way to plant seeds of hope in your life.

**PEOPLE WHOSE WORK STILL
GIVES HOPE TO OTHER PEOPLE**

- _____
- _____
- _____

**HOW I CAN FOLLOW SIMILAR PATHS IN MY OWN
WAY TO PLANT SEEDS OF HOPE IN MY LIFE**

- I can _____
- I can _____
- I can _____

---

was an impact. Yet if Schweitzer had hesitated because he alone could not change the world, there would never have been any change."

Try tackling the exercise called People Whose Work Is Still Alive. Write the names of people who have died but whose contribution still gives people hope. For example: I believe the work of Abraham Maslow, Alexander Calder and Virginia Satir continues to empower people. Describe how you can follow similar paths to inspire both present and future generations. Good models sow seeds of hope in their lives and these often produce harvests in faraway places.

The Ashoka Foundation, The Institute For Social Inventions and The Right Livelihood Foundation, who award the Alternative Nobel Prizes, publicise the efforts of people who create realistic hope. What do such people have in common? Many of them focus on empowering others to shape their own futures.

Children of murderers and murder victims

A.R. Palanisamy is helping the unnoticed victims of murder. Children suffer greatly when a parent kills or is murdered and they enter a world of darkness, loneliness and fear. Pain surrounds the child especially if, for example, the father kills the mother. Where can they go? What help can they obtain? Will they ever be able to create hope in their lives? Palanisamy lives in Tamil Nadu State, where there are 20,000 children at any one time who are secondary victims of murder, while there may be hundreds of thousands across the whole of India. Supported in part by the Ashoka Foundation, he has created a boarding school for 300 such young people, aged between 3 and 20.

Palanisamy believes such children need more than basic care. They need a new source of values and perspective on life. The school provides the students with emotional, academic and practical help.

- The younger students get instruction in spinning, cloth and mat weaving, bag making and sari embroidery.

- The older students take up carpentry, tailoring, horticulture, screen printing and radio repair.

- The students are also helped to find apprenticeships to improve their skills and to earn income.

- The school opens a savings account for each student. The money they earn from work collects interest and becomes theirs when they graduate.

- The school also works to help the children accept their paroled parents. It also helps the reunited family to re-integrate into the community.

Palanisamy was strongly influenced by Gandhi, reports the Ashoka Foundation, which helps him to pass on the message to people in India and around the world.

Children caring for the environment

Ingrid Kavanagh lives in Austin, Texas, but she spent years working in Central America. While in Costa Rica, she introduced the idea of school children volunteering to care for the beaches. Beach clean-ups became popular, spread rapidly throughout Costa Rica and were copied in Honduras. Boosted by the children's enthusiasm, Ingrid formed CAPE (Children's Alliance for Protecting the Environment), whose other projects have included:

- Expansion of the beach clean-up campaign to other countries.

- Sponsorship of co-operative tree-planting programmes for children.

- Promotion of community clean-up and beautification programmes for children.

- Sponsorship of an International Beach Appreciation Day. On a selected date, children all around the world help clean beaches.

- Participation in a Global Clean-Up Party as part of World Environment Week. CAPE has also published a manual describing how children can take part.

Ingrid is empowering children by showing they can shape the future of their world. They can follow their values, set a clear vision and deliver visible results. Having produced tangible successes, such children are more likely to believe they can create their own hope.

YOU CAN HELP PEOPLE TO TAKE CHARGE OF THEIR OWN HAPPINESS

Happiness is a by-product. People enjoy happiness when, for example, they do work they love, help others or follow their life-mission. Combining all three elements often creates a sense of peace. Book stores carry shelves of self-help titles promising instant fulfilment: so can people learn to be happy? Mihaly Csikszentmihalyi believes that people can choose:

a) To do more things that will bring them happiness, or

b) To get more things that they believe will bring them happiness.

Bengt Elmén runs seminars which move audiences to tears. After suffering severe injuries at birth, he now encourages people to do things that will bring them happiness. Oxygen failed to reach the motor cortex area of his brain, causing speech and movement difficulties. Needing constant help to dress, eat and move, Bengt tells audiences how everybody can take a stand toward pain and pleasure in life.

"From the beginning I had to fight for my life," he says. "I was born in Småland, a part of Sweden where people are notoriously stubborn. I learned to be stubborn, to set goals and to manage other people. This was the only way I could survive."

Twenty-five years of struggle saw him graduate from university to become a social worker. Bengt then looked for other challenges. Believing Swedish social care left much to be desired, he built a thriving company which helped disabled citizens to improve their quality of life. As managing director, he saw the company's turnover rise from zero to £5 million per year and employ 800 staff. Bengt then created PEP TALK, which runs seminars for people from all walks of life. A team of personal assistants supports him on stage and translates his words to the audience, which listens to his stories of hope and pain.

"I use humour to show how I have coped with my 'tragic fate', because I want to show that hardships can be seen from two different perspectives," Bengt writes in an article called *What Makes Them Cry?* "After the seminar people find it difficult to complain about trivialities, such as the food being too cold when they go home at night. My positive view shows it is possible to overcome great difficulties, rather than drown in depression, and this is a message of hope and joy. I do not pity myself, so it becomes hard for people to pity themselves. They are forced to look at challenging situations they face in their own lives.

"Humour is something I use to open their senses, to be receptive to other ways of seeing. Laughter also keeps the seminar flowing and boosts the energy level. But my humour must always be relevant and reinforce the message. Life is sometimes tragic, but with every tragedy comes an opportunity for us to learn. This is a message of joy. I believe that people cry on my seminars because they experience both sorrow and joy: the joy of having learned a new way of looking at life."

Life is for living, Bengt says, and he loves life. When tackling the first exercise on one of my workshops, for example, he described his two major passions as: "warm women and cold winters." Overcoming his physical difficulties, he has learned to use his brilliant brain and mischievous sense of humour. Drawing on his own experience, Bengt gives people the following messages during his seminars:

- We are all unique.

- We all have sleeping resources that we can use.

- We can choose our attitude and decide whether or not we want to enjoy life.

- We can choose to do our best to succeed.

- We will find that our attitude decides whether or not we overcome life's challenges.

Bengt inspires people to recognise what Carolyn Simon, a colleague of mine, calls The Second Simplicity. Children see life in simple terms: they believe in love, peace and beauty. Complexity takes over in their early twenties. People learn to speak in long words, take on mortgage debts, seek status and strive to reach a promised Shangri-La. Time brings crises and self-examination. "I'm successful, but I am not happy," somebody says, "I'd like to spend time with my children, do work I love and pass on my knowledge to future generations." Age refocuses our priorities. People often re-invent their lives in their fifties and embrace the values they believed in during their youth. Life calls for caring for our people, products and planet. The Second Simplicity has arrived: but pain and wisdom combine to make this a profound, rather than a naive, simplicity.

Bengt Elmén took responsibility, chose to be enterprising and pursued his life-mission. As a by-product, he also experienced happiness. Travelling this road calls for performing high quality work, which highlights the next step taken by Encouragers.

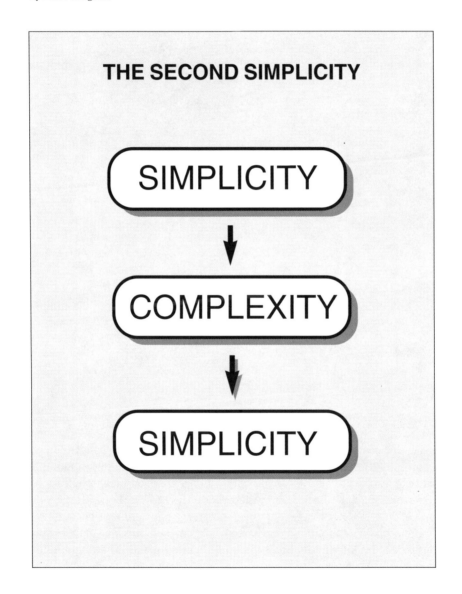

THE SECOND SIMPLICITY

SIMPLICITY

COMPLEXITY

SIMPLICITY

Step Three:
EXCELLENCE

JILL MORRELL did superb work when fighting for John McCarthy's release from captivity in Beirut. Television viewers remember her as the intense woman who, along with a group of dedicated friends, ignored advice from diplomats and kept the hostage issue on the front page. An opinion poll conducted in April 1991, five years after John's capture, showed 91 per cent of the people interviewed recognised his name. A shy person by nature, Jill never saw herself as a heroine or, as other people described her "one in a million".

Eating breakfast on 17 April, 1986, Jill was looking forward to meeting John, who was due to arrive at Heathrow Airport after a one-month assignment in Beirut. His welcome home party at the pub would be followed by a few weeks at work and a holiday in Greece. The telephone rang: it was Roby Burke, a senior manager at their workplace, Worldwide Television News.

"Jill, I have some bad news," said Roby. "John's been kidnapped . . . He was on his way to the airport when some gunmen stopped the car and ordered him out . . . What I need from you is a photograph so that ITN can put it on the lunchtime news."

John was already on the plane, thought Jill; he wasn't valuable to kidnappers. It must be a mistake. Following Roby's instructions, she found a photograph and travelled into WTN. Rumours spread around the office. The British Embassy was pulling out all the stops, but a Lebanese radio station said that John had been executed. Searching for certainty, she rang a journalist based in Beirut, who said: "Forget it love . . . they don't come back." Jill felt angry and powerless.

Writing in *Some Other Rainbow*, Jill explains that she and Nick Toksvig, a friend of John, followed the advice of the experts for the next days, weeks and months. Diplomats stressed it was vital not to rock the boat. Complex political moves were taking place behind the scenes and individual efforts could sabotage the hostage's release. If British diplomacy could not release John, she thought, how could she or Nick succeed? Recalling a visit to the Foreign Office, she writes:

"A guide came to show us the right room and we silently followed her down long corridors, into tiny lifts and past magnificent ante-rooms. It seemed to take ages to get there. As we climbed up a grand, curving staircase past portrait after portrait of former sovereigns and ambassadors, I felt as if I was getting smaller and smaller like Alice in Wonderland, and John's situation less and less important. So many things were going on in the world that needed attention. How much did one person matter to people here?"

Six months of "complex negotiations" produced nothing. Triggered into action by the release of French hostages, Nick and Jill disobeyed the diplomats and set up a fund-raising show at the Comedy Store. ITN picked up the story and highlighted John's plight. Jill, Nick and others then formed the Friends of John McCarthy. Using their creativity to "feed" stories to the media, they made it easy for reporters to publicise the hostage issue. For example, the media preferred to report a hostage spending 300 days in captivity rather than 299. Birthdays and anniversaries were also vital. During the next five years, Jill and her colleagues kept the issue alive by, for instance:

- Holding a press conference to mark John's 300 days in captivity.

- Appearing on television programmes, such as *Wogan*, *Newsnight* and *Heart of the Matter*.

- Placing messages to John in Beirut newspapers.

- Holding an all-night vigil at St. Bride's, the journalists' church in Fleet Street, to mark the first anniversary of John's capture. John later heard of the vigil.

- Setting up a permanent display at St. Bride's and updating it daily to show the number of days John was held in captivity.

- Displaying a huge banner at a World Cup match in Italy. Morocco were playing in the match and it was hoped the banner would be seen by both John and his kidnappers.

- Holding a service at St. Bride's to mark John spending 500 days in captivity.

- Creating a mock-up of John's cell in Covent Garden. Celebrities were invited to spend time sitting in the cell to draw attention to John's captivity.

- Setting up an event called an "Evening Without John McCarthy" at the Camden Palace. This raised £15,000 to continue the campaign.

- Attending the Labour and Conservative conferences.

- Releasing Friends of John McCarthy balloons from the top of Blackpool Tower.

- Holding a 1,000-day vigil outside the Iranian embassy.

- Enlisting the help of the advertising agency Bartle Bogle Hegarty. BBH created huge billboard posters and short films which attracted national attention.

- Getting regular updates of the number of days spent in captivity on such programmes as Simon Mayo's *Radio One Breakfast Show*.

- Launching a Yellow Ribbon campaign to press for John's release. Taxi drivers all over London sported yellow ribbons on their cabs.

John was released on 8 August, 1991. Diplomats and politicians vied to take centre stage, but he owed his freedom to the efforts of the Friends of John McCarthy. Along with this group of dedicated colleagues, Jill did excellent work which eventually produced results. She acted as an inspiring model for others, which is a step taken by many people who are considered to be Peak Performers.

YOU CAN ACHIEVE EXCELLENCE YOURSELF

Everybody has excelled themselves at some time in their lives. Try tackling the exercise called Being Your Best. Describe a time in your life when you did something you believed in, followed a personal dream or overcame a difficult challenge. What did you do right to do your best? How can you follow these paths again in the future? Everybody has a history of successes and has achieved personal or professional excellence

Peak Performers are not extraordinary people. They have a strong sense of mission, however, and do extraordinary things to focus on their values, vision and visible results. Jill Morrell considered herself an ordinary person, but she mobilised all her energy to reach a specific goal. She followed the steps taken by many people who excel themselves.

THEY FOCUS ON THEIR VALUES

Sheila Cassidy, Bengt Elmén and the Ashoka Fellows, for example, were all driven by certain values. Remember when you did something you believed in? You were probably translating your values into action. People do heroic things when they embrace a cause. Such energy can be used creatively or destructively. People risk their lives to save others, strive to create beauty or work to heal the planet. Many also perform courageous acts during wartime.

BEING YOUR BEST

a) Describe a time in your life when you believe you did your best. You may have done something believed in, followed a personal dream or tackled a difficult challenge.

● When I _____

b) What were you doing right then? Write five things you did right to achieve your best.

● I _____

● I _____

● I _____

● I _____

● I _____

c) How can you follow similar paths in the future? Describe three specific things you can do to achieve your best in a particular aspect of your personal or professional life.

● I can _____

● I can _____

● I can _____

THEY FOCUS ON THEIR VISION

Peak Performers translate their values into a clear vision. Jill Morrell had a clear picture: seeing John McCarthy walk free from captivity. Some people start with a vague image which becomes clearer as they strive to reach their goal. "I kept visualising myself running the 400 metres final in many different conditions," said one world champion athlete. "I focused on my own performance in the race, because there was nothing I could do about the other competitors." What happens if every athlete visualises the same race? When everything else is equal, it comes down to will and skill. Attitude plus ability equals achievement.

THEY FOCUS ON THEIR VISIBLE RESULTS

Peak Performers are both Visionaries and Implementers. They master the skills necessary for doing the quality work involved in climbing their chosen mountain. The Friends of John McCarthy, for example, skilfully used the media to keep the hostage issue in the public eye. Peak Performers get the basics right: they do the right thing in the right way every day. They make good use of their own talents and, if necessary, get other people to tackle the

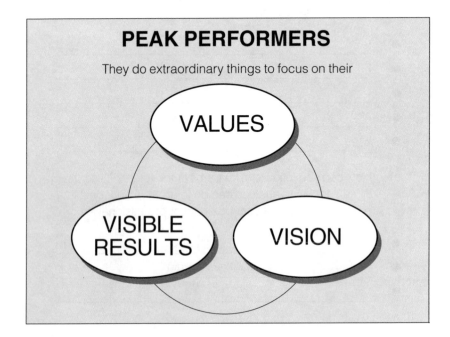

remaining tasks. Keeping their eyes on the mountain top, they are more concerned with long-term goals than short-term feelings. They continue labouring until they stand on the summit of their chosen mountain.

Everybody achieves Peak Performance at some point during their lives. Some people experience this feeling for a few moments, minutes or months. Peak Performers choose to make a lifetime habit of doing extraordinary things to translate their values into a clear vision and produce visible results.

YOU CAN ENCOURAGE PEOPLE TO ACHIEVE EXCELLENCE

Encourage people to do something they believe in. Why? Passion plus Professionalism equals Peak Performance. Joseph Campbell, a professor of mythology, advised his students to "follow their bliss" as the route to finding their life-work. Some felt this gave them permission to drop out and have fun, others felt he helped them to discover how to build a better world. Encourage people to follow their passion in a way that serves other people.

Mary is a school administrator who does work she loves, writes Allan Luks in *The Healing Power of Doing Good*. After completing her day at school, she travels to run a Creative Writing class for inmates at the local prison. She helps the prisoners to develop their skills in spelling, grammar and writing poetry. The classes are voluntary, so it isn't a game for the inmates. They attend Mary's class because they want to learn. She also benefits, saying: "I have been extremely lucky. I feel like I owe something." Allan Luks explains that Mary, like many volunteers, experiences "a transcendent calm" after giving her best.

"On a recent night, driving away from the prison parking lot, she listened to a piece of music by Mozart on the radio and realised that the work she had done with imprisoned people and with others who needed help was her own piece of original music, lifting her own spirits. 'It's for me a creative work. It's a concert.' She could never be a preacher, she said, and she doesn't write as well as she'd like. But she knows how much she can help people, and that feels like a good talent to have."

Giving is a way of receiving. Mary and other helpers enjoy a feeling of optimism about life, writes Allan Luks. He quotes Norman Cousins, who said that: "Altruism is like a muscle." This muscle must be used, because otherwise it withers. Mary and many other carers have found a way to follow their passion.

YOU CAN HELP PEOPLE TO BE PROFESSIONAL

Peter Vidmar, who won the Gymnastic Gold Medal at the 1984 Los Angeles Olympics, describes how people can achieve Peak Performance. He tells conference audiences that gymnasts must first achieve the Olympic Standard of performance to gain a mark of 9.4. They can then add 0.2 by taking a Risk, 0.2 by demonstrating Originality and 0.2 by showing Virtuosity. This produces a perfect 10. Peter is a fine speaker and many people leave feeling inspired, saying, "We can now believe in our dreams, take risks and go for it." Sometimes they forget Peter's most important message: he said that people must first achieve the 9.4. They must work to reach the Olympic Standard in their chosen walk of life, profession or business.

Peak Performers work hard to achieve the 9.4. They do the right thing in the right way every day. Jack Nicklaus, the golfer, began each season by practising his driving, chipping and putting. Great singers, dancers, actors, artists, engineers, sports teams, organisations and companies continually focus on getting the basics right. They practise inner discipline, enjoy the journey and reach the 9.4. Peak Performers practise so that they can forget. They then relax and go for the perfect 10.

How can you encourage people to achieve Peak Performance? They must be using their talents, so begin by giving them the exercise mentioned earlier called My Strengths. People can have all the commitment in the world, but they also need ability to perform outstanding work. Providing they are aware of their talents, you can then guide them through the exercises described on the following pages.

OLYMPIC GOLD	
9.4	OLYMPIC STANDARD
0.2	RISK
0.2	ORIGINALITY
0.2	VIRTUOSITY
10.00	**THE PERFECT TEN**

MY VALUES

Writing in *Build Your Own Rainbow*, Barrie Hopson and Mike Scally, two experts in personal development, underline the importance of people doing something they passionately believe in. Richard Bolles reinforces this point in *What Colour Is Your Parachute*? Both books contain excellent exercises for helping people to follow their values.

My Values is an exercise which invites people to clarify their three key values. Ask them to begin by brainstorming the things they believe in. They may write, for example: "I believe in Love, Freedom, Helping People, etc." Continue until they feel finished, then ask them to choose their top three values. People may be using general statements, but this is okay. They are striving to capture their life-philosophy in a few words. Later on they will focus on how to translate their values into action. Kate, a teacher wrote, for example:

"My three key values are:

● Giving people love.

  Caring for my family, my loved ones and, as far as possible, all other people.

● Giving people beauty.

  Making beautiful products. Creating and delivering superb quality articles, books and courses.

● Giving people hope.

  Doing good work that gives people hope and helps to build a better world."

MY VISION

Peak Performers build on their strengths. This is important to remember when inviting people to clarify their vision. Bearing in mind their talents, what are the three key goals they want to achieve in their life? They may wish to start by brainstorming lots of goals and then choose the top three priorities. Kate said her top two priorities involved caring for her family. The third was: "I want to write a book which shows people how to find positive solutions to conflicts."

MY VALUES

My three key values are:

1) _____

_____

2) _____

_____

3) _____

_____

MY VISION

Three goals I want to achieve in my life

I want to:

1) _____

_____

2) _____

_____

3) _____

_____

MY VISIBLE RESULTS

The specific things I must do to achieve each of my goals:

The goal

1) _____

The specific things I must do to reach this goal are:

● _____
● _____
● _____
● _____

The goal .

2) _____

The specific things I must do to reach this goal are:

● _____
● _____
● _____
● _____

The goal

3) _____

The specific things I must do to reach this goal are:

● _____
● _____
● _____
● _____

MY VISIBLE RESULTS

Visionaries clarify what must be done and Implementers get things done. What must people do to translate their vision into action and produce results? Taking each goal in turn, ask them to brainstorm all the practical things they must do to turn their vision into reality. Kate's plan for writing her book included, for example:

- Set aside time to research the book.

- Research models for finding positive solutions to conflicts. Find success stories in families, workplaces, societies and between nations.

- Develop a model for finding positive solutions to conflicts.

- Decide the target group for the book.

- Find a publisher or plan how to publish it myself. Create a plan for marketing, selling and distributing the book.

- Map out the book.

- Set aside writing time to do the book.

- Write the book. Etc.

Are they prepared to pay the price? Invite people to consider the pluses and minuses of achieving their vision. Maybe they prefer to go for the County Championships, rather than the Olympic Gold. This is okay. It can mean living a more balanced life. People can grow stronger by being honest with themselves and focusing on the real things they want in life. Peak Performers are willing to pay the price for following their chosen path.

YOU CAN ENCOURAGE EXCELLENCE IN EDUCATION

Great educators take three steps towards helping people to develop their talents. Sylvia Ashton-Warner inspired the students to want to learn. She then provided implementation tools that worked and helped the students to integrate the learning into their daily lives. Students must also play their part and practise the right thing in the right way every day. Excellence calls for practising until they forget.

YOU CAN FOCUS ON INSPIRATION

Maria Mendes Abreu inspires teachers to offer imaginative lessons to children in Brazil. Twenty-five per cent of children are illiterate, but politicians still spend only five per cent of the budget on education. Neglect is one reason for illiteracy; another is the poor quality of teacher training, which is mainly theoretical. Teachers entering the classroom for the first time after graduation realise they don't know how to help the students to learn. What do they do? They get the students to repeat or memorise facts without explaining what they mean. Maria believes many children cannot read because teachers fail to make the written word come alive.

The Ashoka Fellowship is sponsoring Maria's teacher re-education programme called "Rever", which means "to look and see again". Starting in the Sao Paulo state school system, she is running three-day reading workshops for teachers. They learn to bring the simplest text to life: to read expressively, pull out key words and help students to speak, write and draw pictures about the book. Children attend the workshop and teachers are helped to correct the children's work without inhibiting their desire to learn. Teachers are also shown ways to create low-cost educational materials from newspapers and magazines. Ashoka reports:

"'We help the teachers find the child in themselves,' says Maria. Not surprisingly, bringing children into the workshops daily to test out the methodology helps demonstrate its effectiveness to participants. 'The kids are what gives credibility to the project,' she says."

Maria aims to reach all 4,000 primary teachers in Sao Paulo. How? She began by training five people to run reading workshops for teachers. She is now devoting a year to educating a core group of "multipliers" to run workshops for more "multipliers", thereby spreading waves of learning across the city. Maria is a public entrepreneur who ignites the flame of imagination in teachers and, she hopes, in children. After changing the Sao Paulo system, she plans to take the workshops to other cities across Brazil.

YOU CAN FOCUS ON IMPLEMENTATION

Mohammed Zakaria offers implementation tools to village people in the southern delta of Bangladesh. Villagers must develop analytical skills and have a sense of "ownership" in planning their futures, he believes, otherwise they stand little chance of long-term survival and success. An Ashoka Fellow, Mohammed helps the poorest villagers to collect their own data, develop their own overall plan for the area and then make it happen. He hopes this

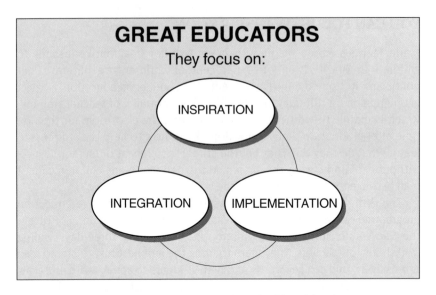

grass-roots initiative will create a new breed of local leaders sensitive to their villages' special needs.

How does this work in practice? Mohammed starts by inviting a group of likely future village leaders to focus on key themes and to ask basic questions. After getting people to make a map of their village, he asks them questions such as:

- How much food does the village need?

- How much did it need in 1972 after independence?

- How much will it need in 2000?

- Is rice alone enough for a healthy diet?

Villagers analyse whether or not the land available can produce the food they need to feed their people. If not, new questions emerge, such as: What other alternatives are possible? How can we generate other forms of income? What skills must we learn to reach our goals? Six to twelve months may pass before a practical consensus plan of action emerges, says Mohammed, but it is then owned by the villagers. He provides people with 100 basic questions that help them gather and analyse the data they need to tackle their challenges. Villagers can then continue to use these questions to shape their own futures.

"Mohammed focuses on young working people 20-45 years old, having found them flexibly open to change and of an age to assume leadership in the near future," says the Ashoka report. "Although he is working with 45 villages, he's giving most of his attention to ten of these. That's a large enough field to give his approach a broad test, under different circumstances, yet it's still manageable."

One key point on implementation. Mohammed prefers working with the bottom 60 per cent of a village, the people who control relatively few of the village's resources. Why? They must become active and develop their own economic base. Success will develop their confidence to withstand pressures from élites both inside and outside the village. Mohammed is following the path taken by many great teachers who give people practical implementation tools. He is empowering people to shape their own future.

YOU CAN FOCUS ON INTEGRATION

Great educators help people to integrate the learning into their daily lives and ensure it becomes what psychologists call an "unconscious competence". People integrate learning on different levels. Touch-typing becomes part of somebody's life through constant practice. Driving a car becomes second nature; people often drive on auto-pilot when speeding along the motorway. "Human skills" can be more difficult to learn, however, because they call for discarding old habits.

My Right Book encourages people to develop their human skills by recording their achievements (see next page). "But I don't do anything well," somebody may argue. They probably do thousands of small things right each day and such actions contain the seeds of their successful patterns. People grow by recognising and repeating what works. Dave, a social worker, wrote:

a)   Three things I have done right today

- I helped Josie, aged 8, to move in with her new foster parents. I met her early in the morning to describe the plans for the day, confirmed she still wanted to move to the family and drove her to the house. I spent the first hour with Josie to make sure she settled into the family, handed her my phone number and set a time to visit her next week.

- I refused to bow to threats from Derek, a drug addict, who wanted me to provide him with money. I offered an alternative by saying I would help him to find a job he liked.

- I encouraged one my of colleagues who is going through a difficult divorce. I spent time with her at lunch, gave her a chance to talk, and discussed how she and her partner could do the best for their children.

b) **Two things I can do even better tomorrow**

- I can structure my time better. For example: Spend the first hour doing paper work and organise home visits so I am not dashing from one end of town to the other. If it suits people, I can arrange my schedule so that I visit clients who live in the same district during the same block of time. I can also set up self-help groups so people support each other rather than continually relying on me.

- I can look after myself better and do something I enjoy tomorrow evening.

MY RIGHT BOOK

THREE THINGS I DID RIGHT TODAY

- I _____

- I _____

- I _____

TWO THINGS I CAN DO EVEN BETTER TOMORROW

- I can _____

- I can _____

People integrate new skills by building on what works and tackling areas for improvement. Eugen Herrigel described the pain and pleasure of this quest for integration in his classic book *Zen in the Art of Archery*. Daisetz Suzaki, writing in the Foreword, explains: "If one really wishes to be master of an art, technical knowledge of it is not enough. One has to transcend technique so that the art becomes an 'artless art' growing out of the Unconscious."

Suzaki describes the integration process on a spiritual level: "In the case of archery, the hitter and the hit are no longer two opposing objects, but are one reality. The archer ceases to be conscious of himself as the one who is engaged in hitting the bull's-eye which confronts him. This state of unconscious is realised only when, completely empty and rid of the self, he becomes one with the perfecting of his technical skill, though there is in it something of a quite different order which cannot be attained by any progressive study of the art."

Eugen spent the first year learning to place himself in the background. His master told him to "relax", to let the arrow fire itself. Eugen writes: "When, to excuse myself, I once remarked that I was conscientiously making an effort to keep relaxed, he replied: 'That's just the trouble, you make an effort to think about it. Concentrate entirely on your breathing, as if you had nothing else to do!'"

After several years Eugen learned to relax his body until the moment of the bow's release. Those few successful shots taught him to understand what was meant by drawing the bow "spiritually". Like many seekers, however, he fell victim of his own desire to reach his goals.

One summer holiday Eugen discovered a technical way to fire the arrow. Cautiously easing the pressure of the fingers on the thumb, a moment came when the thumb was torn out of position by the tension in the bow. Virtually every shot went off smoothly and he convinced himself he was on the right track. The technical solution might become a habit and "spiritualize itself". Returning from holiday, Eugen proudly demonstrated his progress to the Master.

"The very first shot I let off after the recommencement of my lessons was, to my mind, a brilliant success. The loose was smooth, unexpected. The Master looked at me for a while and then said hesitantly, like one who can scarcely believe his eyes: 'Once again, please!' My second shot seemed to me even better than the first. The Master stepped up to me without a word, took the bow from my hand, and sat down on a cushion, his back towards me. I knew what that meant, and withdrew."

Eugen's shame turned to horror: the Master refused to teach a "cheat".

Apologies and pleas led to the Master relenting. Lessons recommenced from the beginning and all previous learning was discarded. Eugen still searched for an intellectual secret, however, plying the Master with questions about when "It" would shoot. The Master's reply was simple: "Don't ask, practise." Months passed and one day, after a shot, the Master bowed and ended the lesson, saying: "Just then, 'It' shot!" Eugen stared at him bewildered and then cried out with delight. This led to a severe rebuke.

"'What I have said', the Master told me severely, 'was not praise, only a statement that ought not to touch you. Nor was my bow meant for you, for you are entirely innocent of this shot. You remained this time absolutely self-oblivious and without purpose at the highest tension, so that the shot fell from you like a ripe fruit.'"

Eugen began to release more right shots and recognise the successes. He graduated to the next stage, shooting at a target. Previous years had been devoted to one thing: learning how to release the arrow. Time passed and one day the Master cried out immediately the shot was loosed: "It is there! Bow down to the goal!" Eugen was disappointed to see the arrow had only grazed the edge of the target. The Master rebuked him, telling him to forget the target and saying: "You must practise unceasingly — you cannot conceive how important it is." Practise he did, and Eugen finally learned the "artless art". Talking with the Master one day, he tried to make sense of what happened. Did he hit the goal or did the goal hit him?

"Bow, arrow, goal and ego, all melt into one another, so that I can no longer separate them. And even the need to separate has gone. For as soon as I take the bow and shoot, everything becomes so clear and straightforward and so ridiculously simple."

Not everybody wants to become a Zen master; but excellence calls for repeated practice: Practising so that you can forget.

YOU CAN ENCOURAGE EXCELLENCE IN WORK

Peak Performers flow, focus and finish. "Sometimes I experience 'white moments'," said one athlete. "Everything clicks. My skills and the challenges I face come together in a feeling of complete harmony. Years of training pay off. Everything seems perfect and things are easy to achieve." Like many things that sound simple, such effortlessness seldom comes easily. Let's explore some ways you can help people to make full use of their talents.

YOU CAN HELP INDIVIDUALS TO ACHIEVE EXCELLENCE

Peak Performers have a healthy attitude to both successes and setbacks. They use both as the springboard to improving their future performance. Sports activities often show people at their best and this is one reason why individuals and companies, for example, are learning from sports people. Writing in *The Mental Athlete*, Kay Porter and Judy Foster, describe a series of interviews they had with Olympians. Elite athletes intuitively created their own mental training programmes. The skills they had in common were:

- They frequently recalled their own past powerful performances. They recalled these in great detail and focused on how to follow similar patterns in future events. They then visualised their future performance for days or weeks before the event.

- They had total concentration and focus during the competition. They had a total belief in themselves and their physical abilities. They kept following their successful patterns, especially in the most critical times of the event.

- They continued to see themselves as winners, even after losing a competition or two. They analysed both successes and setbacks to improve their performance, techniques or strategy. They looked forward to new challenges and were easily able to let go of defeats.

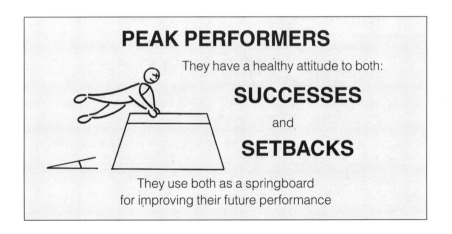

PEAK PERFORMERS

They have a healthy attitude to both:

SUCCESSES

and

SETBACKS

They use both as a springboard
for improving their future performance

My Success is an exercise which, like many others in this book, invites you to learn from your own experience. Begin by recalling one of your own outstanding achievements. What did you learn from your success? What did you do right to do your best? Sports people who do this exercise try to be extremely specific by focusing on every aspect of their preparation and performance. After clarifying what you learned from your achievement, plan how to apply these lessons in the future. You can also use this information for rehearsing, or visualising, your future performance.

MY SUCCESS

1) Write one outstanding success that you have achieved in your life.

My success

● _____

2) Write three things that you learned from the success.

I learned

● _____

● _____

● _____

3) How can you use what you learned? Write three things you can take from what you learned and apply these things in the future.

● I can _____

● I can _____

● I can _____

LEARNING FROM SETBACKS

Peak Performers' ability to learn from setbacks is a key factor that distinguishes them from other people. Sheila Cassidy was imprisoned and tortured in Chile, but emerged to work with dying patients. Jill Morrell was shocked by John McCarthy's capture, but used her energy to fight for his release. Sebastian Coe, the favourite, failed dismally in the 1980 Olympics 800 metres final, but bounced back one week later to win the 1,500 metres Gold Medal. Bengt Elmén suffered damage at birth, but urges people to take charge of their lives. Setbacks provide something more than immediate pain: they can help us to find our real work in life.

Mihaly Csikszentmihalyi studies people who find their life mission. They take certain steps towards fulfilling their mission, vocation or life purpose, he says. These include:

First: People have a profound experience and translate this into a positive challenge.

They experience something which has a great impact on their lives. Sometimes it is one of pleasure, more often it is one of pain. Virginia Satir, for example, suffered a severe illness and spent months in hospital. She returned home to find the family in chaos. Her mother cut off her hair and Virginia became deaf. She took the next step which such people have in common.

They decide to do something to improve the situation. Virginia learned to lip-read and found other ways to get close to people. She also began growing and selling plants to earn money. She decided that, when she grew up, she would be a "children's detective", which had something to do with unravelling puzzles.

Second: People set themselves a goal, work hard and get positive results.

They have a dream and, over the next months or years, they formulate this into a specific goal. Virginia eventually decided to help people by becoming a psychiatric social worker. She kept re-clarifying her aims and moved on to helping whole families. Such people stride towards a hazy mountain top and waft away the clouds until they see a crystal-clear goal.

They follow their vocation, experience both successes and setbacks, and reach their goal. Virginia helped many families and then moved on to training family therapists. She also produced several books which communicated her message to both therapists and families. Virginia then took the next step which is a characteristic of many people who pursue their life mission.

Third: People widen their work into a mission to help others and build a more Positive Planet.

They want to offer something to all humanity. Encouragers often do this in a humble way, placing themselves in the background and seeing

---

MY SETBACK

1) Write down one setback that you have experienced in your life.

My setback

● _____

2) Write three things that you learned from the setback.

I learned

● _____

● _____

● _____

3) How can you use what you learned? Write three things you can take from what you learned and apply these things in the future.

● I can _____

● I can _____

● I can _____

---

themselves as servants. Virginia Satir remained grateful for all the love she had been given and wanted to pass this on to both present and future generations. "She was focused on helping the world in both the present and future," writes Laurel King in *Women of Power.* Virginia herself added:

"I realised that my whole career in the healing profession was to create a condition where people could have two things — health and peace . . . If anything gets done in this world, it's because human energy does it. More and more I think we in this world are getting the message that we don't have to wait for somebody to tell us it's okay. All you have to do is put one foot in front of the other. If we can send men to the moon, we can find ways to live happily with one another. I know that."

My Setback is an exercise you can use to clarify what you have learned from a difficulty. Go as deep as you wish with the exercise. Some people focus on a childhood illness, severe rejection or other crisis. Other people focus on a failed work project, poor performance or hardship. What did you learn from your setback? How can you apply this learning in the future? You may or may not find the roots of your life mission when doing the exercise, but it can provide valuable lessons for tackling your next setback.

YOU CAN HELP TEAMS TO ACHIEVE EXCELLENCE

Peak performing teams flow, focus and finish. The Brazilian football team won the 1970 World Cup by combining teamwork with magnificent individual performances from players such as Pele. They enchanted crowds and lifted people out of their seats. The Beatles enjoyed a magical period when, guided by Brian Epstein, they combined their talents to produce superb songs. Mihaly Csikszentmihalyi reports that other teams enjoy a sense of flow.

"Surgeons say that during a difficult operation they have the sensation that the entire operating team is a single organism, moved by the same purpose; they describe it as a 'ballet' in which the individual is subordinated to the group performance, and all involved share in a feeling of harmony and power."

Great teams give people a glimpse of paradise. Earlier in the book we looked at positive teams. Peak performing teams are different, they ascend into another dimension. If you wish, tackle the exercise on the next page which invites you to look at Super Teams. How do they make magic, not once, but time and time again? Such teams follow The Organic Way, rather than The Oppressive Way, a philosophy we will explore later in the book.

Super teams tend to focus on their strengths, specific goals, strategy, support and success. Let's explore what a good coach does when taking over a football team. Although a sports example, you can follow similar principles in any form of teamwork.

SUPER TEAMS

1) Write the names of three teams that you believe have done superb work and created a sense of magic. These can be in sport, the arts, business or any walk of life.

- _____
- _____
- _____

2) Did these teams have any things in common? Try to find things they had in common and write what you believe they did right to create magic.

- They _____
- They _____
- They _____
- They _____
- They _____

3) How can your team follow these steps in its own way? Write three concrete things your team can do to make magic.

- We can _____
- We can _____
- We can _____

YOU CAN CLARIFY THE TEAM'S STRENGTHS

Good coaches begin by watching the football team play in a practice game. They watch for when the team flows. When does it come alive? When does it work best? When does it create magic? They look for people's individual and collective strengths. Good coaches spot the team's natural successful patterns. What are the natural combinations between people? What are people doing right? What can they do better and how? You can apply this approach in your own team by tackling the exercise on the next page called My Team's Strengths Inventory. It is vital to build on these strengths when clarifying your strategy for reaching your goals. Football is a simple game: it involves people combining their talents to reach an agreed goal, which highlights the next step.

YOU CAN CLARIFY THE TEAM'S SPECIFIC GOALS

Good coaches inspire people to put their hearts and souls into achieving common goals. How to make this happen? They begin by winning people. They make training enjoyable, build alliances with key players and tell people they will build on their strengths. They then describe the team's aims. Coaches cannot play the games, however, so they give people a sense of ownership and gain their commitment to reaching the goals. How? One way is to outline the goals and the benefits for the players. Players will later be given an opportunity to suggest their ideas for implementing the strategy.

"Sport is just about winning, but working life is much more complicated," a person may argue. Goals in sport can also be complex, because they must mirror the club's philosophy. Does the club want its players to express their talents or to win at all costs? Does it want to serve the local community or to foster élite athletes who compete at national level? Does it want to combine both philosophies? Ten years ago I coached the youth team of a Second Division football club in Sweden. Our three goals were:

- To have a positive attitude.

- To play positive football.

- To get positive results.

Pursuing these principles called for taking tough decisions, such as only

MY TEAM'S
STRENGTHS INVENTORY

Many teams get hooked on creating a Problem Inventory. This exercise turns that approach on its head. While it is important to clarify areas for improvement, begin by clarifying your strengths. List all of your team's assets, knowledge, skills, experience, resources, contacts, etc. It will be vital to build on these strengths when clarifying your strategy for achieving success.

1) _____

2) _____

3) _____

4) _____

5) _____

6) _____

7) _____

8) _____

9) _____

10)_____

selecting players who had a good attitude. Footballers must encourage their team-mates, especially during crises. They must take responsibility for their own actions, rather than blame the referee, the pitch or outside events. Players who chose to behave in a different way were given 24 hours to change. Sounds tough? Maybe, but the club believed in these principles. Security is to have an alternative, so I had already recruited five fine players who wanted to join the team. It wasn't a tragedy when the star centre forward chose to leave.

Clarifying the team's strategy is a vital step. Good coaches do this by returning to the concept of flow. After agreeing on the team's goals, they consider the players' individual and collective strengths. They ask: "How can we co-ordinate our strengths to reach the goals?" Football calls for scoring more goals than the other team. It also calls for doing all the practical tasks — such as attacking, defending, etc. — and giving everybody a chance to be creative. Such challenges are similar to those facing people in a shop, factory or any other workplace. The key question is: "How can we combine our talents to reach all our personal and collective goals?"

Good coaches communicate the strategy to the players and gain their commitment to reaching the goals. How? One way is to invite the players to consider the suggested playing style (be it 3-5-2, 4-3-3 or whatever) and explore the pluses and minuses of this style. The game plan is given but, within this framework, people can make suggestions for improvement. Players must believe in the strategy and know their part in making it happen, because they will be the ones to bring it alive on cold winter afternoons. Good coaches conclude any discussions by inviting the whole team to commit themselves to working hard to reaching the goals.

YOU CAN OFFER THE TEAM SUPPORT

Good coaches get the right balance between structure, support and spontaneity. How? They spend hours on the training ground getting the players to practise the team's set moves. Footballers must be willing to follow the agreed patterns, but they must also know when to break free and use their skills in critical areas of the field. Great players are those that dare to do things, rather than don't do things. They create magical moments that bring joy to spectators. Good coaches have individual discussions with each player to agree on their role in the "Game Plan" and the support they need to do the job. Clear contracts are made with each player, who is offered the opportunity to "be creative within parameters".

IN ENCOURAGE THE TEAM TO DO SUPERB WORK

Good coaches fulfil their part of the contract. They encourage, educate and equip their players to achieve positive results. Providing everybody does their best, the team will achieve success. Sometimes they will flow. The Swedish youth team played a semi-final match, for example, in which we were trailing 1-2 with only 20 minutes left on the clock. Moving a key player into mid-field changed the chemistry of the game. Suddenly our players started passing the ball crisply. Events on the field appeared to be going slowly and yet swiftly. Months of practice paid off and the team entered a different world. We scored three goals during the next 15 minutes and won the match 4-2.

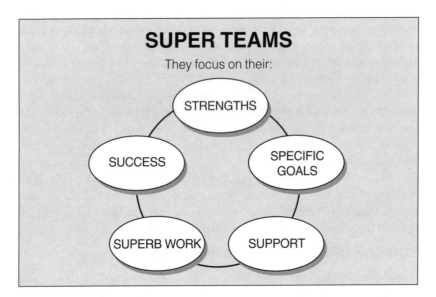

YOU CAN GUIDE THE TEAM TO SUCCESS

Good coaches encourage players to finish. This always means following certain life principles and, as a result, sometimes means winning trophies. They help players to build on their strengths, manage pressure and become the best kind of team they can be. Great athletes thrive on stress. They see it as an opportunity to go into what sports people call "The C Zone": they become Calm, Controlled and Centred. Good coaches help their players to learn how to finish and, as a by-product, to achieve ongoing success.

"You can guarantee style. You can't guarantee results," said Glenn Hoddle, a gifted footballer who gave pleasure to millions of spectators. In 1983 he led Swindon Town to promotion in a play-off at Wembley. They went 3-0 up against Leicester City but then conceded three quick goals. The score was 3-3 and Leicester were rampant. Hoddle rallied his players, saying: "Keep playing football. It is 0-0. We can do it." His players returned to following their principles and won 4-3. Swindon Town may never again reproduce that form, but for one shining afternoon they shared the experience of many other creative teams. They tasted the joy of being able to flow, focus and finish.

People can follow these principles to build excellent teams. If you wish, tackle the exercise called My Super Team, which focuses on specific things you can do to build a great team. Like the Brazilian football team and The Beatles, however, such teams frequently do their best work over a short period of time. People find it much harder to build organisations that continue to achieve Peak Performance.

MY SUPER TEAM

Try tackling this exercise which focuses on specific issues your team can address on the way towards reaching its goals. The next step is to implement these ideas and guide your team to success.

STRENGTHS

Write your team's three main strengths.

- _____
- _____
- _____

SPECIFIC GOALS

Write your team's three main goals.

- _____

- _____
- _____

SUPPORT

Write the specific things you can do to offer support to your team.

- _____
- _____
- _____

SUPERB WORK

Write the specific things you can do to ensure your team does superb work.

- _____
- _____
- _____

SUCCESS

Write the specific things you can do to ensure your team achieves success.

- _____
- _____
- _____

YOU CAN HELP ORGANISATIONS TO ACHIEVE EXCELLENCE

Great organisations clarify their values, translate these into a vision and produce visible results. The Quakers, The Body Shop, Amnesty International, Comic Relief, The Mothers of the Disappeared and The Friends of John

McCarthy have all attracted admiration because they stuck to their beliefs, especially during times of crises. Peak performing organisations start by focusing on the principles that inspire people to get out of their beds in the morning.

VALUES

"Sports Hotels wants to write a values statement," said Lynn, the managing director. "Companies often print their values on plastic cards but fail to live the message. We want to bring our values to life. Can you help us?"

"Are you serious?" is the first question to ask leaders when they plan to launch any initiative. Many senior teams feel good about producing a new value, mission or vision statement. Only 1 in 20, at most, are willing to pay the price involved in translating their fine words into action. Sports Hotels believed in caring for its staff, but what did this mean in practice? It might mean giving the staff a profit share. "No problem," said Lynn. "This may be necessary if we are to inspire our staff to do their best." Maybe they were serious.

Sports Hotels' senior team tackled several exercises geared to translating their values into action. They started by asking themselves: "What are our three key values?" One hour later they agreed on their priorities. They wanted to build a caring company. Sounded good, but could they deliver? Senior managers often write lovely words without realising the consequences of living the message. Lynn's inner cabinet were inviting criticism. Firing a negative employee, for example, could be interpreted as being cruel. They explored these issues and confirmed the company's values. (Every employee needed to "own" these values, so later it would be vital to involve all staff in shaping the final values statement.) Lynn's team declared:

We Want:

- To care for our customers.

- To care for our colleagues.

- To care for our cash.

Caring for people sounds idealistic, but Ricardo Semler, President of Semco, has shown that it works, writes Charles Garfield in *Second To None*. Taking over a near bankrupt company in 1980, Ricardo helped it to become one of Brazil's most admired and profitable companies. Semco, which makes equipment for the marine and food processing industries, opted to encourage its people. "We wanted a company that prospered because we could count on the people, not because we controlled every move they made," said Ricardo. Semco hires people who have a history of taking responsibility in their homes and local communities. "We start from a few basic assumptions, says Ricardo. "First of all, we only hire responsible adults." By having high standards and caring for its people, Semco finds that people care for the company.

VISION

Great organisations translate their values into a clear vision. Lynn's team needed to get a picture of the future company. What would Sports Hotels look like if they lived the values? What would be the consequences? Were they willing to pay the price? They tackled the exercise called Values In Action, which focuses on the specific steps they could take to translate their beliefs into behaviour. (You may wish to try this exercise in your own organisation.) Exploring their second value, "To care for our colleagues", the senior team's suggestions included:

- Reward the behaviour we want repeated. Promote people who are good people-managers. Evaluate managers' performance on their ability to encourage people and produce team results.

- Invite staff to suggest concrete ways to improve the company. Follow the LEAD model when responding to their ideas. Listen, evaluate and act on the suggestions. Show goodwill by implementing at least 80 per cent of the suggestions.

Listen
Evaluate
Act
Deliver

● Introduce a company-wide profit share. Employees might then ask senior managers awkward questions, such as: "How much money are you making sitting in all these management meetings?" "Is it necessary for all of you to attend?" and "Shouldn't you be out selling?" But having a profit share will create greater business awareness.

VALUES IN ACTION

Begin by writing your organisation's three key values. Continue by writing the specific things it can do to translate these values into action.

The first value

1) _____

The specific things we can do to translate this value into action are:

● _____

● _____

● _____

● _____

● _____

The second value

2) _____

The specific things we can do to translate this value into action are:

● _____

- _____
- _____
- _____
- _____

The third value

3) _____

The specific things we can do to translate this value into action are:

- _____
- _____
- _____
- _____
- _____

Peak Performers accept the price involved in reaching their goals. Sports Hotels' senior team tackled this issue by doing the exercise called Are You Serious? They asked: "What will be the consequences of living the values? What will be the pluses and minuses for the customers, the staff, the middle managers, the senior managers and the company?" Lynn's colleagues were surprised to find that most of the minuses involved themselves as a Board. While remaining answerable for the company's financial results, they must stop supervising and continue to develop their role as Coaches. They concluded the session by asking themselves: "Bearing everything in mind: Are we serious? Do we really want to translate the values into action?"

VISIBLE RESULTS

Great organisations keep their promises. They do what they say they will do. Sports Hotels' senior team focused on how to get some early wins. They introduced the LEAD programme and implemented 80 per cent of the staff's suggestions. "Employees believe what they see, not what they hear," said Lynn, "which is why we produced some quick successes. Leaders must also learn to follow. Listening and leading calls for a fine balance, but it is the best way to build the business. Providing the ideas are well thought out, we must implement at least 90 per cent of the staff's ideas for improving Sports Hotels."

ARE YOU SERIOUS?

How serious is your organisation about living its values? Before publishing a values statement, or launching any other initiative, it is important to explore the consequences of translating your words into action. You can do this by listing the pluses and minuses of living your values: for the customers, staff, middle managers, senior managers and the organisation.

	PLUSES	MINUSES
FOR THE CUSTOMERS	● _____ ● _____ ● _____	● _____ ● _____ ● _____
FOR THE STAFF	● _____ ● _____ ● _____	● _____ ● _____ ● _____

FOR THE
MIDDLE
MANAGERS

● _____   ● _____

● _____   ● _____

● _____   ● _____

FOR THE
SENIOR MANAGERS

● _____   ● _____

● _____   ● _____

● _____   ● _____

FOR THE
ORGANISATION

● _____   ● _____

● _____   ● _____

● _____   ● _____

FOR ANY
OTHER GROUPS

● _____   ● _____

● _____   ● _____

● _____   ● _____

Bearing these things in mind, do your really want to live your values? If so, make specific plans for translating your values into action. Go for some quick wins and produce visible successes.

Ricardo Semler helped the Semco staff to make the company profitable by taking steps which other companies find too radical. Grand phrases about people being their greatest asset mean nothing. Companies must develop or die. They must put their money where their mouth is and, if they are serious, focus on encouragement. Semco took the following steps towards becoming successful:

- They reduced the management layers from 11 to 3. They set up business units of around 150 people. When the unit reached 200-250 people they broke it up into two units. This kept the focus on people rather than numbers.

- They encouraged every Semco business unit to set its own strategies. People were also asked to set their own salaries, develop their own profit-sharing programme and decide how to distribute this profit share. Semco encouraged a philosophy of paying people according to their value to the company, rather than their seniority or status.

- They created self-managing teams and gave them clear parameters within which they could make their own decisions. They introduced flexitime and encouraged people to set their own working hours and factory schedules. They stopped having security room padlocks and audits for petty cash.

- They set up regular meetings to handle any abuses of the flexitime or production problems. That was years ago and they are still waiting for their first meeting to be called to handle problems.

Semco has become both admired and profitable, but Ricardo believes that people must retain a sense of what is really valuable in life. Leaders must balance the demands of caring for their people, profits and planet. He writes:

"I spend much of my time travelling around the world and finding ways to preserve the Brazilian rain forest, and it makes me realise that we need a sense of preservation. We are doing things at a tremendous speed, things that are all very short-term decisions. Tremendous companies and tremendous efforts are reduced to dust, sometimes in a decade or two or three.

"I think the lesson from the rain forest is that it is not worth it for mankind to be constantly tearing away things that were the root of its existence, just to generate short-term results. I think we end up using short-term decision-making as a substitute for understanding much more complex issues, which include our place in the world as a whole."

YOU CAN ENCOURAGE EXCELLENCE ACROSS THE PLANET

Ricardo Semler pursues a path taken by many people who work to build a better world. Viktor Frankl, George Lyward and Virginia Satir also belonged to a certain tradition. Such people follow The Organic Way, rather than The Oppressive Way. They love life, build on people's strengths and encourage diversity. Recognising the real meaning of education, Sylvia Ashton-Warner helped people to develop their talents. Richard Bolles and Paul Hawken help people to do meaningful work during their lives on Earth.

Peak Performers also follow The Organic Way. Nurturing their inner gifts, they develop the discipline required to achieve excellence. Pele called football "the beautiful game" and Brazil's 1970 World Cup team were described as: "Playing football as if they came from another planet." They actually followed the best life principles on this planet. Getting the perfect balance between structure and spontaneity, they combined their talents to make magic. Sport, the arts and creativity can show people at their best and leave spectators with a tempting glimpse of paradise.

Ricardo Semler, Sheila Cassidy, the Ashoka Fellows and many others believe that we belong to one world. Millions of people must "own" this view before we can guarantee a better world for our children. How to make this happen? "Show rather than tell" is one way. It is best to lead by example. People must be offered good models, see the benefits and choose to care for the planet.

One further complication: people cannot be coerced into making this choice. They must actively choose to follow this philosophy in an organic, rather than oppressive way. Why? While we must make laws to protect the planet, for example, people must then develop the Zen Master's inner discipline to translate these values into daily action. Good educators point the way to nurturing this inner discipline. They make inspiration, implementation and integration the three stages on the journey towards achieving excellence.

THE ORGANIC WAY	THE OPPRESSIVE WAY
Loving life	Fearing life
Encouraging people	Disqualifying people
Building on people's strengths	Putting people in organisational boxes
Encouraging diversity	Suppressing diversity
Believing in education	Believing in schooling
Creating meaningful work	Maintaining boring work
Developing an economy to serve the people	Making people serve the economy
Promoting co-operation	Promoting competition
Creating Win-Win	Creating Win-Lose
Developing inner discipline	Relying on outer discipline
Balancing short and long-term planning	Going for short-term gain
Applying holistic thinking	Applying reductionist thinking
Working for sustainable development	Working for growth at all costs
Living in harmony with nature	Destroying nature
Building a positive planet	Patching up a troubled planet

YOU CAN FOCUS ON INSPIRATION ACROSS THE PLANET

Jean Giono chose to inspire people by writing a parable called *The Man Who Planted Trees*. One day in 1913 he was walking in the barren wilderness at the foot of the Alps in Provence. Searching for water, he met a 50-year-old man called Elzeard Bouffier, who invited him to have supper at his stone house. Having once owned a farm in the lowlands, the man had lost both his wife and son. Elzeard now cared for his lambs and dog but feared the land was dying for lack of trees, so he devoted his days to restoring life to the wilderness. He believed that, if God granted him thirty more years, he could plant enough oak trees, beech trees and birch trees to bring life and fertility to the soil. Jean stayed overnight and the next day accompanied the shepherd on his mission.

"He began thrusting his iron rod into the earth, making a hole in which he planted an acorn; then he refilled the hole. He was planting oak trees. I asked him if the land belonged to him. He answered no. Did he know whose it was? He did not. He supposed it was community property, or perhaps belonged to people who cared nothing about it. He was not interested in finding out whose it was. He planted his hundred acorns with the greatest of care."

Saying "Good-bye" to the shepherd, Jean returned home to serve as an infantryman in the 1914-18 World War. Five years later he decided to revisit the barren lands of Provence. Elzeard was still alive and so was the countryside. Oak trees formed a small forest; beech trees grew as far as the eye could see; birch trees were taking root in the valleys. Creation caused a chain reaction. The wind scattered seeds across the land and water flowed through the streams. Success brought its own problems. Some years later the Government placed this "natural forest" under their protection and warned Elzeard against damaging the trees. Jean talked with a friend in the Forest Service, however, and ensured that Elzeard was allowed to pursue his mission. One day they travelled to see the fruits of his labour.

"In the direction from which we had come the slopes were covered with trees twenty to twenty-five feet tall. I remembered how the land had looked in 1913: a desert . . . Peaceful, regular toil, the vigorous mountain air, frugality and, above all, serenity of spirit had endowed this old man with awe-inspiring health. He was one of God's athletes. I wondered how many more acres he was going to cover with trees."

Elzeard Bouffier died peacefully at a hospice in Banon in 1947, writes Jean. But he didn't, of course, because he only lived in the pages of the book and the film called *The Man Who Planted Trees*. Jean ran into difficulties with his American editors, writes Norma Goodrich in the Afterword to the book. Why? In 1953 they asked him to describe an unforgettable character. He chose to describe somebody who would be unforgettable. When the editors discovered that no "Bouffier" had died in the shelter at Banon, a tiny mountain hamlet, he looked elsewhere to publish the story. It was accepted by *Vogue* and appeared in March 1954 as *The Man Who Planted Hope and Grew Happiness*.

Jean Giono's story quickly spread around the world. Like the seeds in Elzeard's imaginary barren land, it created life and gave people hope. His purpose in creating Bouffier was to make people love trees or, more precisely, to make them love planting trees, writes Norma Goodrich.

Jean believed he left his mark on earth when he wrote Elzeard Bouffier's story, saying: "It is one of my stories of which I am the proudest. It does not bring me in one single penny and that is why it has accomplished what it was written for." Artists had a crucial part to play in building a better world, Jean felt, and his story aimed to inspire a tree-planting programme that would renew the Earth.

Elzeard Bouffier may have been fictional, but Richard St Barbe Baker, the International Tree Foundation and the Green Belt Movement in Kenya have all done real work to nurture life on Earth. Who knows where the seed came from to inspire these people to care for the planet?

YOU CAN FOCUS ON IMPLEMENTATION ACROSS THE PLANET

Lynchburg College inspires its students to develop both personal and professional excellence. By getting students to move beyond classroom theory, it encourages them to become implementers who focus on the human application of knowledge. Located in the foothills of Virginia, USA, Lynchburg asks all 2,500 students to do voluntary work in the local community. Young people who get the chance to serve others feel valuable and develop as whole human beings, say Allan Luks and Peggy Payne in *The Healing Power Of Doing Good*.

George Rainsford, Lynchburg's president, says the volunteer programmes play a vital part in preparing students for the 21st century. The college has a moral obligation to educate young people to be contributors in a world which will have five characteristics. He believes the world:

- Will be racially diverse.

- Will be highly technological.

- Will be one which involves international partnerships.

- Will be one which requires co-operation to achieve solutions.

● Will be one where public service will be in the best
   interests of both the individual and the community.

Lynchburg introduces students to community service in their first week
at the college. They are then given the message: "This is a part of college life,"
says Rosemary Urban, who co-ordinates the programme, "It isn't something
they're tacking on; it's built in." Special attention is paid to helping the
young people to use the strengths they bring to the voluntary work.
Lynchburg students are placed in situations where they can help others,
grow in confidence and succeed. "The key word is need," says Rosemary
Urban, "giving them an opportunity to be needed."

Good teachers educate the heart and the head. Humanity must balance
its moral development with its material and technical development to build
a better world. Young people in particular have great energy and idealism.
Students can be given the chance to help others and discover that Givers can
also become Receivers. Caring for others helps us to heal ourselves, because
we are one body and belong to one world.

"Make Money, Have Fun, Do Good," is the recipe for good work, says
Joline Godfrey in her book *Our Wildest Dreams*. She describes the journey
taken by many women implementers who are running businesses. A fresh
view of work is emerging and it is based on humanistic principles. People
want to combine the best of work and family, rather than be forced to make a
"No Win" choice. They are seeking both quality of life and quality of work.

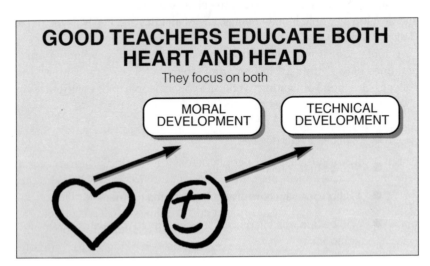

**GOOD TEACHERS EDUCATE BOTH
HEAD AND HEART**

They focus on both

MORAL DEVELOPMENT   TECHNICAL DEVELOPMENT

Joline kicked herself into action one day after reading an article about talented entrepreneurs. The magazine prided itself on being in touch with the times, but failed to mention any women in its all-male Dream Team. She contacted the editor, who acknowledged the mistake and suggested she write a feature article about women running successful businesses. Joline responded with a suggestion of her own. The magazine could help her to travel the country, meet women and create a resource bank which reporters could use for future stories. The editor backed her plan and one of the results was *Our Wildest Dreams*.

"How did you start?" was one of the questions she asked the women. Joline explains three main ways that they launched into running a particular business.

1) They followed a dream or simply got inspired.

2) They adopted a business. Some women inherited, bought, or otherwise took over an existing business. Sometimes a business gets adopted because, in the quest to survive, it is the only opportunity that presents itself.

3) They responded to perceived needs and market opportunities.

"My greatest triumph has been to do exactly what I wanted to do with my life and make a business out of it," one woman told Joline, adding: "I continue to think that it is extraordinarily valuable that women hold on to the sense that their lives are a whole lot more than their work, their careers, and their businesses."

Our Wildest Dreams has helped many people to make the transition from vision to action. Women are skilled at juggling family life and work, says Joline, and can enjoy the best of both worlds. By describing the paths taken by good models, she shows how people can turn their dreams into reality. Joline continues to write, speak and encourage people on a practical business level. Balance is vital, however, and her motto remains: "Make Money, Have Fun, Do Good".

Bill Mollison has inspired people across the world by introducing a permanent form of agriculture called Permaculture. We already know how to solve every food, clean energy and shelter problem, he says. The planet gives us all the answers and we do not need to re-invent the life principles. Watching which birds are dispersing seeds of useful forest trees, for example, shows that this process can be encouraged to promote reafforestation. Seeing what works in nature, we can apply the lessons to feed, clothe and house everybody on the planet. Bill writes:

"What we have done, we can undo. There is no longer time to waste or any need to accumulate more evidence of disasters; the time for action is here. I deeply believe that people are the only critical resource needed by people. We ourselves, if we organise our talents, are sufficient for each other. What is more, we will either survive together, or none of us will survive. To fight between ourselves is as stupid and wasteful as it is to fight during times of natural disasters, when everyone's co-operation is vital."

Permaculture is based on watching how natural systems work and evolve. We can learn from them, apply the learning and develop ways in which:

- To provide people with their basic needs, such as food, energy and shelter.

- To provide a natural and self-sustaining way to integrate agriculture with the environment.

Co-operation, not competition, is the basis of existing life systems, says Bill. It is also the basis for our survival. Peace and conflict start with the questions we ask, because a question can be asked in two ways. For example: "What does this person, or land, have to give if I co-operate with them?" or "What can I get from this land, or person?" The first question leads to peace and plenty; the second to war and waste. Co-operation calls for our respecting "The Law of Return", says Bill. Whatever we take, we must return. He adds: "Every object must responsibly provide for its replacement; society must, as a condition of use, replace an equal or greater resource than that used."

Embracing the "Seventh Generation" concept will help us safeguard the future, says Bill. The American Indians (Iroquois nation) believe today's decisions must be based on the benefits or losses for our descendants in seven generations' time (about 100 years ahead). He adds: "The only ethical decision is to take responsibility for our own existence and that of our children." Bill believes we must encourage diversity, rather than suppress it. Diversity has much to teach us and may provide the key to our own survival. People can use their differences creatively to restore and nurture our beautiful earth.

"Great changes are taking place," says Bill. "These are not as a result of any group or teaching, but as a result of millions of people defining one or more ways in which they can conserve energy, aid local self-reliance, or provide for themselves. All of us acknowledge our own work is modest; it is the totality of such modest work that is impressive."

Permaculture has proved successful in thousands of places around the world. Bill has given people a philosophy and practical methods that work, but he remains realistic about changes he will witness in the future.

"I do not, in my lifetime, or that of my children's children, foresee a world where there are no eroded soils, stripped forests, famine, or poverty, but I do see a way in which we can spend our lives towards Earth repair. If and when the whole world is secure, we have won a right to explore space, and the oceans. Until we have demonstrated that we can establish a productive and secure earth society, we do not belong anywhere else, nor (I suspect) would we be welcome elsewhere."

Bill Mollison, Joline Godfrey and the Lynchburg teachers chose their way to be Implementers. You may wish to tackle the exercise on the next page called My Tradition. Who are the people you admire? Whose path do you want to follow in your way? For example, my own models are people such as Abraham Maslow, Virginia Satir, Viktor Frankl, Sheila Cassidy, Sylvia Ashton-Warner, Richard Bolles and Bernard Benson, author of *The Peace Book*. Why? They each wrote books which gave a new view of people's possibilities. They were realistic Utopians who showed how to build a Positive Planet. While not having the same talent as these people, I can follow their steps in my own way.

People who find their tradition recognise they are part of something greater than themselves. They feel part of a river which has been flowing for many years and will continue to flow after they die. Feeling both humbler and stronger, they can simply do their best while they are on Earth. What is your tradition?

YOU CAN FOCUS ON INTEGRATION ACROSS THE PLANET

Christopher Alexander urges us to take to heart the wisdom of our world. A pioneering architect by profession, his ideas can be used in many fields of work. Writing in *The Timeless Way of Building*, he declares: "Each one of us has, somewhere in his heart, the dream to make a living world, a universe." Architects nurse this desire at the centre of their lives, says Christopher. One day, somewhere, somehow, they want to create a building which is wonderful, a place where people can walk and dream for centuries. Every person has some version of this dream. Some wish to create a house, a garden or a fountain. Others wish to create a relationship, a painting or a book.

MY TRADITION

1) What is your tradition? Who are the people you admire? Write the names of the people, living or dead, whose path you would like to follow in your own way.

- _____
- _____
- _____

2) What do you admire about these people? What did they do well? Write five things you believe they did well to do good work during their lives.

- _____
- _____
- _____
- _____
- _____

3) How can you follow their path in your own way? Write three things that you can do in your own life or work.

- I can _____
- I can _____
- I can _____

The "Timeless Way of Building" has always existed, says Christopher. It inspired the building of traditional villages of Africa, India and South America; the building of great religious monuments; the mosques of Islam, the temples of Japan. It inspired the simple benches, cloisters and arcades in English country churches; the mountain huts of Norway and Austria; the bridges of the Italian middle ages; and the cathedral of Pisa. It inspires a person, a family or a town to be alive and it gives birth to many forms of creative life. The "Timeless Way" can be recognised but is hard to name. And yet people are born with the ability to create this sense of wonder, says Christopher.

"In the world of living things, every system can be more or less real, more true to itself or less true to itself . . . This oneness, or the lack of it, is the fundamental quality for any thing. Whether it is in a poem, or a man, or in a building full of people, or in a forest, or a city, everything that matters stems from it. It embodies everything.

"The word which we most often use to talk about the quality without a name is the word 'alive'.

"Things which are living may be lifeless; non-living things may be alive. A man who is walking and talking can be alive; or he can be lifeless. Beethoven's last quartets are alive; so are the waves at the ocean shore; so is a candle flame; a time may be more alive, because more in tune with its inner forces, than a man."

Words such as "free", "whole" and "eternal" can also describe the Timeless Way, says Christopher. Language is helpful but can also be limiting. Surprised by joy, your whole being suddenly recognises freedom and beauty. Flow experiences don't just happen, however, they can be created.

Like many arts, learning the Timeless Way of Building calls for mastering and then shedding a discipline. Christopher moves from the philosophical to the practical, and his book describes the specific things architects can do to shape buildings which inspire people to be creative. People other than architects can apply similar ideas. He says:

"The search we make for this quality, in our own lives, is the central search of any person, and the crux of any individual person's story. It is the search for those moments and situations when we are most alive."

The Japanese film *Ikuru*, to live, describes the life of an old man who discovers he is to die of stomach cancer in six months, says Christopher. Having spent the previous 30 years sitting behind a counter and stopping his dreams surfacing, the man seeks to enjoy life. He seeks pleasure but cannot find satisfaction. Finally, against all obstacles, the man helps to build a park in a Tokyo slum.

"He has lost his fear, because he knows he is going to die," says Christopher." He works and works and works; there is no stopping him, because he is no longer afraid of anyone, or anything. The man no longer has anything to lose and so, in a short time, he gains everything; and then dies, in the snow, swinging on a child's swing in the park he has made, and singing."

A circus family of high-wire artists once had a terrible fall, says Christopher, maiming or killing all of them except the father. The old man escaped with broken legs, and a few months later returned to perform on the high wire. Why? The father answered: "On the wire, that's living . . . all the rest is waiting."

Christopher asks the reader: What is your high wire? When do you feel most alive? Like living on the cliff-edge or falling in love, such golden moments are the times when we feel most right, most just, most sad and most hilarious. They are the special, secret moments in our lives when we smile unexpectedly, says Christopher, who adds:

"A woman can often see these moments in us, better than a man, better than we ourselves even. When we know those moments, when we smile, when we let go, when we are not on guard at all — these are the moments when our most important forces show themselves; whatever you are doing at such a moment, hold on to it, repeat it — for that certain smile is the best knowledge that we ever have of what our hidden forces are, and where they live, and how they can be loosed."

Recognising this quality in ourselves, we can also recognise it in our surroundings, says Christopher. Nature is never the same, but it contains common patterns and individual variations, endless repetition and endless variety. While the patterns are repeated, the variations are unique. When the spider builds its web, the process is standardised, but the parts created are all different. Each web is beautiful, unique, perfectly adapted to its situation. Architects can learn these secrets, says Christopher, who describes specific ways they can create wonderful buildings. Inviting us to search for integration, he concludes *The Timeless Way* by writing:

"Almost everybody feels at peace with nature: listening to the ocean waves against the shore, by a still lake, in a field of grass, on a windblown heath. One day, when we have learned the timeless way again, we shall feel the same about our towns, and we shall feel as much at peace in them, as we do today walking by the ocean, or stretched out in the long grass of a meadow."

PEOPLE CAN BUILD A POSITIVE PLANET

Pearl and Samuel Oliner have handed down a challenge to humanity in their book *The Altruistic Personality*, which chronicles the activities of people who protected Jews during the Holocaust. Up to 500,000 non-Jews risked their own lives to rescue the victims of Nazi persecution. They were "ordinary" people, say Pearl and Samuel: farmers, teachers, entrepreneurs, factory workers, rich and poor, parents and single people, Protestants and Catholics. Different people helped the Jews in different ways. Some offered them shelter; some helped them escape from prison; some smuggled them out of the country. The "Rescuers" showed that people can do wonderful things, even in the midst of catastrophe.

"Paradoxically, confronting goodness may be more painfully challenging than confronting evil," writes Harold M. Schulweis, in the book's Foreword. "Would I rescue a pregnant woman, a hungry and homeless child, an aged, frightened couple — provide them with food and shelter, dispose of their refuse, and care for them in their sickness — knowing that doing so might bring disaster upon my family and myself from Nazi pursuers and their informers?"

Madness stalked Europe but there remained shining examples of humanity. Rescuers committed themselves to helping Jews, knowing that capture would mean death for their families. Why? Many had loving backgrounds. Louisa, a Rescuer, says: "My mother influenced me mostly by love. She was a warm woman, and we admired her for her wit, her wisdom, and her intelligence. She was our friend and we could confide in her."

Some Rescuers had close connections with Jews before the war; others had strong moral beliefs and translated their love into action. War shows people at their best and worst, say Pearl and Samuel. *The Altruistic Personality* describes people who had the courage to care.

Sheila Cassidy, Bengt Elmén, Viktor Frankl and millions of ordinary people have also chosen to do their best. Writing in *Sharing the Darkness*, Sheila remembers: "I recall the young Catholic woman dying of cancer who asked me one day, 'How can I use my suffering for others?'"

What do you want to do? If you wish, tackle the exercise My Action Plan. How do you want to use your life-experience? How do you want to pass on your wisdom? How do you want to plant seeds of hope during your life? Write three things you can do to encourage other people.

Sports people sometimes say: "Will plus Skill can Thrill". Athletes must have the will to succeed before they can apply their skills and thrill the audience. Do you have the will to achieve what you have written? Rate the probability out of 10 of your doing each of these things. Be realistic when making action plans. Start by doing something where you can give yourself at least a 9 out of 10 chance of reaching the goal.

MY ACTION PLAN

How do you want to pass on your life-experience and wisdom? Write three specific things you want to do to encourage people. Then rate the probability, out of ten, of doing each of these things.

1) _____

   _____

The probability of my doing this is.............../10

2) _____

   _____

The probability of my doing this is.............../10

3) _____

   _____

The probability of my doing this is.............../10

People can take responsibility for using their talents. At its deepest level, this calls for living in "good faith". Writing in *The Fall*, Albert Camus outlines the challenge facing each of us. One night a sailor walks across a bridge and passes a man who is looking down into the river. Suddenly there is a splash. The sailor doesn't look back. He pauses, thinks and walks on. From that night on the sailor's life is dogged by bad luck: he loses friends, money and his job. Reflecting on that crucial moment, the sailor longs to return and grasp a second opportunity. Surely he would dive into the river and save the drowning man. "Ah, but the water is cold," he says to himself. The sailor knows what he should do, but avoids taking responsibility. We each cross our individual bridges every day. By choosing to live in "good faith", we can do what is needed to care for the Seventh Generation.

People can combine their talents to build a better world. As the Zen Master told Eugen Herrigel, we can practise every day of our lives. Practice makes perfect. We can practise encouragement, practise enterprise and practise excellence. Like Peak Performers, we can practise until we forget. Paradoxically, however, we must never forget. Providing we have the will, we can get to the 9.4 and reach the perfect 10. Providing we do our best, we will often catch a glimpse of paradise. People can earn an Olympic Gold by building a Positive Planet.

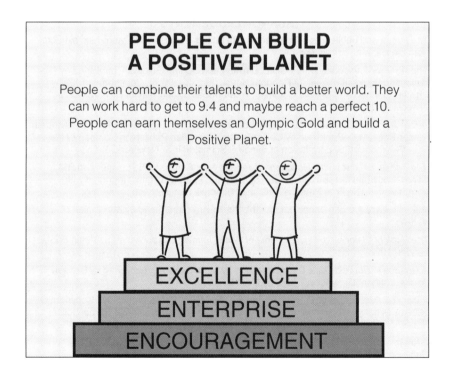

PEOPLE CAN BUILD
A POSITIVE PLANET

People can combine their talents to build a better world. They can work hard to get to 9.4 and maybe reach a perfect 10. People can earn themselves an Olympic Gold and build a Positive Planet.

EXCELLENCE

ENTERPRISE

ENCOURAGEMENT

CONCLUSION

I have been very fortunate during my life. Given a loving start by parents who adopted me, I have been supported by superb teachers. Many other inspirers have been people I never met. They shared their wisdom by doing good work or by making beautiful products. "My thoughts are a collection of other people's flowers," somebody once wrote, "and I have merely provided the string." Accept this book in the same spirit. Pick the flowers you like best and arrange them in your own bouquet.

"What can I do to help to build a better world?" I once asked one of my teachers. "If I can only do one thing, what do you suggest I do?"

"Be an Encourager," she replied. "Encourage one person and they are more likely to encourage another. The seeds will blossom and spread around the world. If you only do one thing in your life, be an Encourager."

ACKNOWLEDGEMENTS

The author and publishers acknowledge with thanks permission to reproduce extracts from the following publications:

The Ageless Spirit edited by Phillip L. Berman and Connie Goldman, published by Ballantine Books, a division of Random House, Inc., New York. Copyright © 1992 by Philip L. Berman and Connie Goldman. Reproduced by courtesy of Richard Curtis Associates, Inc., New York.

AIDS: The Ultimate Challenge by Elisabeth Kübler-Ross. Copyright © 1987 by Elisabeth Kübler-Ross, M.D. Published by Collier Books, Macmillan Publishing Company, New York. Reproduced by permission of Simon & Schuster, Inc., New York.

The Altruistic Personality: Rescuers of Jews in Nazi Europe by S.P. Oliner and P.M. Oliner. Copyright © 1988 by Samuel P. Oliner and Pearl M. Oliner. Reprinted with permission of The Free Press, a division of Simon & Schuster, Inc., New York.

References to Ashoka, Innovators for the Public, are reproduced by permission of Ashoka.

The Book of Visions: An Encyclopedia of Social Innovations published by Virgin Books, London 1992.

A Chance to Serve by Alec Dickson (edited by Mora Dickson), published by Dobson Books, London. Copyright © 1976 by Mora Dickson.

Flow: The Psychology of Optimal Experience by Mihaly Csikszentmihalyi. Copyright © 1990 by Mihaly Csikszentmihalyi. Excerpts reprinted by permission of HarperCollins Publishers, Inc., New York.

Growing a Business by Paul Hawken, published by Simon & Schuster, Inc., New York. Copyright © 1987 by Paul Hawken.

Photograph: Philip Price

MIKE PEGG

Mike Pegg lives near Ross-on-Wye and has spent the past 30 years working as an Encourager. Leaving school at 15, he spent six years on a factory assembly line before Community Service Volunteers gave him the opportunity to help other people. He went on to run therapeutic communities for young people, qualifying as a psychotherapist and teaching family therapy.

During the 1970s he ran Encouragement Workshops throughout Europe, as a result of which he was invited to train business leaders, government decision-makers and national sports teams. He now works with TMI, a leading training consultancy company, specialising in helping people who want to achieve and maintain peak performance. His clients include Sony, Lunn Poly, Air Miles, the Dorchester Hotel and the Young President's Organisation.